H. Montagu (Henry Montagu) Villiers

Corpus Christi: a manual of devotion for the Blessed Sacrament

H. Montagu (Henry Montagu) Villiers

Corpus Christi: a manual of devotion for the Blessed Sacrament

ISBN/EAN: 9783742840738

Manufactured in Europe, USA, Canada, Australia, Japa

Cover: Foto ©Thomas Meinert / pixelio.de

Manufactured and distributed by brebook publishing software
(www.brebook.com)

H. Montagu (Henry Montagu) Villiers

Corpus Christi: a manual of devotion for the Blessed Sacrament

CORPUS CHRISTI

A Manual of Devotion for the
Blessed Sacrament.

WITH A PREFACE BY

THE REV. H. MONTAGU VILLIERS

VICAR OF ST. PAUL'S, WILTON PLACE

'The Bread which we break, is it not the Communion
of the Body of Christ?'

RIVINGTONS
WATERLOO PLACE, LONDON
MDCCCLXXXIV

In

Thankfulness to GOD

for

The Life and Teaching

of

WILLIAM JOSIAH IRONS,
Priest,

Who entered into Rest,

June 18, 1883.

Lord, now lettest Thou Thy servant depart in
peace : according to Thy word.
For mine eyes have seen : Thy salvation.

PREFACE.

IT is a revealed truth that 'man shall
not live by bread alone,' that the soul
of man requires food for its sustenance
suitable to its spiritual needs, that it cannot rest in the finite, that the Living GOD
must be the support of a living soul.
Our LORD'S teaching was founded on
this principle when He said, 'Except ye
eat the Flesh of the SON of Man, and
drink His Blood, ye have no life in you.'

The saying was a hard one, and
difficult to understand—as the disciples
found it ; but to limit the truths of Religion to those which we can perfectly
understand is rationalism.

The Catholic Church, striving to live
by 'every word that proceedeth out of
the mouth of GOD,' teaches us that this

nourishment of the soul is afforded to us in the Eucharist, and that after the consecration of the Bread and Wine, our LORD JESUS CHRIST, both GOD and Man, is truly, really, and substantially present under the species of those sensible things, and that thus GOD is brought down to us, and by our acts of Communion becomes one with us and we with Him, —a doctrine which is quite independent of the further question of transubstantiation, or the change of the substance of the Bread and Wine.

But the Eucharist is not only a means of bringing GOD down to us, it is a means whereby we ascend to GOD ; and so again the Church teaches us that the Precious Body and Blood being there sacramentally under those outward forms, are through them offered to the FATHER as the Great Memorial Sacrifice,—the Memorial before GOD of that Sacrifice offered once for all upon the Cross. The devotions contained in this Manual will be found to embody these precious truths.

It has been asked where in the present

day we find such calm, deep minds, dwelling in the invisible and rapt in heavenly things, ever facing eastward amidst the whirl of life, as were found in times gone by. I will not take upon myself to reply to the question, but I recommend this little book the more heartily because so many of its devotions sprang from those 'calm, deep minds,' and reflect their earnestness. It will have its own interest to many to know that several of the prayers are from the old Sarum Missal (so dear to all English Catholics), for leave to publish which, as here translated, the compiler is indebted to Mr. Harford Pearson.

In the arrangement of this Manual there is much that is new and original, in its matter there is much that is old and venerable, and it will be found suggestive with thoughts drawn from the piety of all ages,—thoughts with which we may well examine ourselves before we presume to eat of that Bread and drink of that Cup (*v.* Pt. I.); thoughts with which we may well be armed when we venture to unite with beings above ourselves in the scale of creation, and with Angels and Archangels, and with all the company of Heaven, to laud and magnify the glorious Name (*v.* Pts. II. and III.) ; and finally, thoughts with which we may guide the expressions of our grateful hearts when we re-echo in Thanksgiving the Angels' song, 'Glory be to GOD on high, and in earth Peace, good will towards men (*v.* Pt. IV.).

That GOD may bless this endeavour of one whose earnest wish it has been to assist others both in their Communions and in their Worship, is my sincere prayer in heartily recommending this little Manual. May He grant to those who use it unity, a true faith, and a life agreeable to His Holy Will.

H. MONTAGU VILLIERS.

F. S. Michael and All Angels,
1883.

I will be sanctified in them that come nigh Me, and before all the people I will be glorified.

NOTE.—*The Devotions in Parts I. and IV. are divided into portions which may be used at discretion. It should, however, be borne in mind that Self-Examination is a necessary part of preparation for Holy Communion. No form of questions for that purpose has here been given, as it seems superfluous to add to those already in existence.*

It may be mentioned that the Psalms and other portions of Holy Scripture which are given in this book are intended to be dwelt upon devotionally as meditations, and are not to be used merely as prayers or readings.

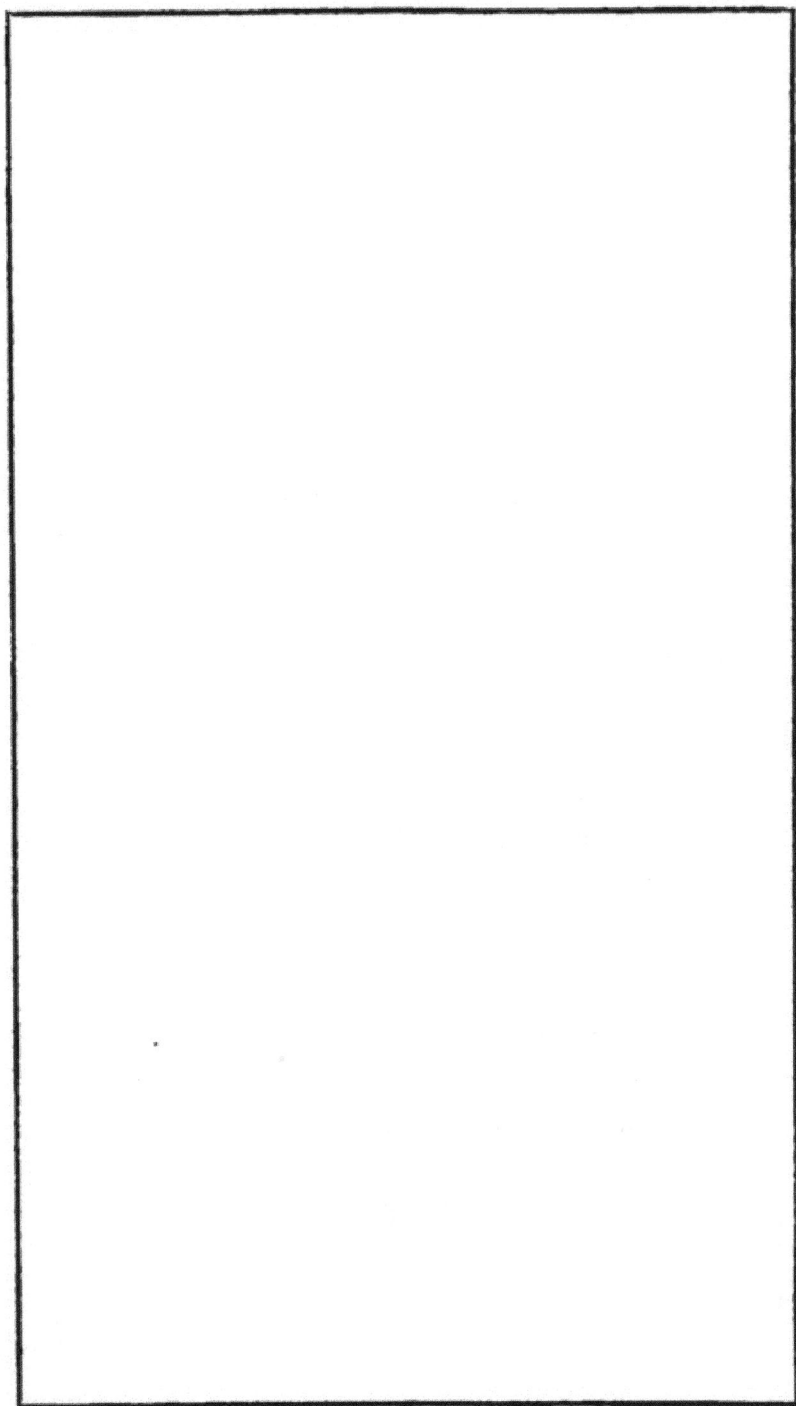

CONTENTS.

PART I.

PREPARATION.

PART II.

PART III.

PART IV.

THANKSGIVING, ETC.

Preparation for Holy Communion.

Remember the words of the LORD JESUS how He said,

Whoso eateth My Flesh and drinketh My Blood hath Eternal Life, and I will raise him up at the Last Day. . . . He that eateth My Flesh and drinketh My Blood dwelleth in Me, and I in him. . . . As I live by the FATHER, so he that eateth Me, even he shall live by Me. . . . Abide in Me, and I in you.

Be diligent that ye may be found of Him in peace, without spot, and blameless.

Self-Examination.

Let a man examine himself, and so let him eat of that Bread and drink of that Cup.

IN the Name of the ✠ FATHER, and of the SON, and of the HOLY GHOST. Amen.

Righteousness, O LORD, belongs unto Thee, but unto me confusion of face, a weak, vain, and sinful child of man.

I am not worthy of the air I breathe, of the earth I tread upon, or of the sun that shines upon me ; much less worthy to lift up either hands or eyes unto Heaven.

For Thou hast said that no unclean thing shall come within Thy sight ; and how then shall I appear who am so miserably defiled ?

O my GOD, Thou madest me of nothing, and Thou seest how I have spoiled this work of Thine, for I am still in my sins, and what to do I know not.

But this I will do ; I will confess my

wickedness, and be sorry for my sin ; I will not suffer mine eyes to sleep, nor mine eyelids to slumber, until I have, by the mediation of Thy dear SON, earnestly besought Thy pardon.

Therefore now, LORD, I pray Thee, call my sins to my remembrance ; and when Thou hast done so, blot them out of the Book of Thy remembrance, and pardon me.

Then say the following.

COME, HOLY GHOST, our souls inspire,
    And lighten with celestial fire.
Thou the anointing SPIRIT art,
Who dost Thy seven-fold gifts impart.

Thy blessed Unction from above,
Is comfort, life, and fire of love.
Enable with perpetual light
The dulness of our blinded sight.

Anoint and cheer our soiled face
With the abundance of Thy grace.
Keep far our foes, give peace at home :
Where Thou art Guide, no ill can come.

Teach us to know the FATHER, SON,
And Thee, of Both, to be but One.
That, through the ages all along,
This may be our endless song ;

Praise to Thy eternal merit,
FATHER, SON, and HOLY SPIRIT.

In the sight of GOD *and of the Holy Angels, examine your conscience, and confess your sins.* (See Note to Part II.)

I CONFESS to Almighty GOD, before the whole company of Heaven, that I have sinned exceedingly in thought, word, and deed, through my own most grievous fault. [*Here mention the particulars.*] For these and all my other sins, which I cannot now remember, and for all the sins which I have at any time committed [*Here think of the chief sins of your life*], I am heartily sorry, firmly purpose amendment, and most humbly ask of GOD pardon for all my sins, and grace to amend my life for the time to come.

A PRAYER OF S. ANSELM.

O MOST High and Most Gentle Lover of men, to Thee I confess all my sins, whatsoever and howsoever committed, from the hour when I first could sin, up to this hour, in which, by Thy Mercy, Thou still sufferest me to live. Before Thy Majesty and before all Thy Saints, I confess that I am guilty, and worthy of punishment, and that unless Thy Mercy come to my aid, I must be condemned to everlasting death, and utterly perish from Thee.

Have mercy upon me, O LORD, who cry unto Thee ; let the voice of faith weeping to Thee move Thy Love ; and let that Mercy, in which alone I hope, forbid Thee to be extreme to mark that which I have done amiss. I know that unless Thou forgive, Thou mayest justly punish me ; but with Thee is much compassion and abundant propitiation.

Grant then, O most Loving FATHER, that what I have done, I may bewail ; and in Thy Love deign to keep me free from all attacks of the Evil One, that henceforward I may serve Thee in righteousness and peace, and may live before Thee.

Grant me to avoid and to conquer all snares and temptations and hurtful delights, and perfect in me a complete obedience to Thy Blessed Will. Give me humility and piety, discreet abstinence and mortification of the flesh,—a pure and sober and devout mind, intent only upon serving Thee, and delighting in Thy commandments. Give me ever, O LORD, with humility to advance to better things, and never to sink back. Free Thou me from all evils, and bring me to Life Everlasting.

Behold, O LORD, my Light and my Salvation, I have laid before Thee what I fear, I have asked what I need, and all my hope is in Thy wonderful great Mercy

in CHRIST JESUS.   For His sake I entreat
Thee, hear me now.

May the Almighty and Merciful LORD
grant unto me absolution and remission
of all my sins, to the Glory of His Holy
Name, and the salvation of my soul.
Amen.

PSALM CI.   𝔐isericordiam et judicium.

MY song shall be of mercy and judgment : unto Thee, O LORD, will I
sing.

O let me have understanding : in the
way of godliness.

When wilt Thou come unto me : I will
walk in my house with a perfect heart.

I will take no wicked thing in hand ; I
hate the sins of unfaithfulness : there shall
no such cleave unto me.

A froward heart shall depart from me :
I will not know a wicked person.

Whoso privily slandereth his neighbour:
him will I destroy.

Whoso hath also a proud look and high
stomach : I will not suffer him.

Mine eyes look upon such as are faithful
in the land : that they may dwell with me.

Whoso leadeth a godly life : he shall be
my servant.

There shall no deceitful person dwell
in my house : he that telleth lies shall not
tarry in my sight.

I shall soon destroy all the ungodly that are in the land : that I may root out all wicked doers from the city of the LORD.

Glory be to the FATHER, and to the SON : and to the HOLY GHOST ;
As it was in the beginning, is now, and ever shall be : world without end. Amen.

BENEDICTION

To be used at the end of any of these Devotions.

MAY the Faith of the Holy TRINITY and the Incarnation of CHRIST, the Power of the Cross and the Virtue of the Sacraments, be unto me life, redemption, glory, and grace, this day and for evermore. And may the Blessing of GOD Almighty, the ✠ FATHER, the SON, and the HOLY GHOST, be with me and with mine now and at the hour of death. Amen.

Desire for Communion.

We would see JESUS.

MY soul is athirst for GOD, yea, even for the living GOD; when shall I come to appear before the Presence of GOD?

O that I knew where I might find Him, that I might come even to His Seat!

Tell me, O Thou Whom my soul loveth, where Thou feedest, where Thou makest Thy Flock to rest?

Thus saith the high and lofty One that inhabiteth Eternity, Whose Name is Holy—

'I dwell in the high and holy Place, with him also that is of a contrite and humble spirit, to revive the spirit of the humble, and to revive the heart of the contrite ones.'

'I, even I, will both search My sheep and seek them out; I will feed them in a good pasture; I will feed My Flock, and I will cause them to lie down. Thus shall they know that I, the LORD their GOD, am with them.'

Who, O LORD, will grant me this, that
I may find Thee only, and that Thou alone
mayest speak to me and I to Thee,—as
he who loves speaks with him who is
loved, and friend with friend?

For this I long, for this I pray,—that I
may be united wholly to Thee, and that I
may detach my heart from all worldly
things, and that through Holy Communion,
and frequent worship there, I may more
and more delight in Heavenly and Eternal
things.

Give me, I beseech Thee, wings of contemplation, that clothed in them I may fly
up to Thee.   Hold Thou my heart in Thy
Hand, for without Thee it is not drawn to
higher things.   Thither I would fain hasten,
where Perfect Peace reigneth, and Everlasting Tranquillity is bright,—even to the
Altar of Thy Sacrament, the Tabernacle
of Thy Rest, my King and my GOD.

At Thy command, O LORD, let all things
be hushed to me, that I may know how
great is the abundance of Thy Sweetness
which they enjoy who love nought, desire nought, so much as Thee.   O happy
they whose only Hope Thou art, and all
their work is praise!   Blessed is the man
whose strength is in Thee, in whose heart
are Thy ways.

When I shall with my whole self cleave
to Thee, I shall nowhere have sorrow or

labour; and my life shall wholly live as wholly full of Thee. For Thou hast made us for Thyself, and our heart is restless till it finds its rest in Thee.

O that I might repose in Thee! O that Thou wouldest enter into my heart and fill it with joy, that I may forget my ills, and embrace Thee, my Sole Good! Behold, LORD, my heart is before Thee; open Thou the ears thereof and say, I am thy Salvation. After this Voice let me haste and take hold of Thee. Hide not Thy Face from me. Let me die—lest I die—only let me behold Thy Face. LORD, I beseech Thee, shew me Thy Glory!

Thus saith the LORD—
'I will meet with thee, and I will commune with thee from above the Mercy-Seat.'
'I will see you, and your heart shall rejoice, and your joy no man taketh from you.'

PSALM XLII. Quemadmodum.

LIKE as the hart desireth the water-brooks : so longeth my soul after Thee, O GOD.

My soul is athirst for GOD, yea, even for the living GOD : when shall I come to appear before the Presence of GOD?

My tears have been my meat day

and night : while they daily say unto me, Where is now thy GOD?

Now when I think thereupon, I pour out my heart by myself : for I went with the multitude, and brought them forth into the house of GOD ;

In the voice of praise and thanksgiving : among such as keep holy-day.

Why art thou so full of heaviness, O my soul : and why art thou so disquieted within me?

Put thy trust in GOD : for I will yet give Him thanks for the help of His countenance.

My GOD, my soul is vexed within me : therefore will I remember Thee concerning the land of Jordan, and the little hill of Hermon.

One deep calleth another, because of the noise of the water-pipes : all Thy waves and storms are gone over me.

The LORD hath granted His lovingkindness in the day-time : and in the night-season did I sing of Him, and made my prayer unto the GOD of my life.

I will say unto the GOD of my strength, Why hast Thou forgotten me : why go I thus heavily, while the enemy oppresseth me?

My bones are smitten asunder as with a sword : while mine enemies that trouble me cast me in the teeth ;

Namely, while they say daily unto me :
Where is now thy GOD ?

Why art thou so vexed, O my soul : and
why art thou so disquieted within me ?

O put thy trust in GOD : for I will yet
thank Him, Which is the help of my
countenance, and my GOD.

Glory be to the FATHER, and to the
SON : and to the HOLY GHOST ;

As it was in the beginning, is now, and
ever shall be : world without end.   Amen.

Self=Oblation.

Greater love hath no man than this.

O HEAVENLY FATHER! for His dear sake Who came to fulfil Thy Will for us, even our Redemption, have mercy upon me, Thy slothful, unworthy, unholy servant.

He pleased not Himself, but taking upon Him humility,—that is, the likeness of sinful flesh,—He loved His Own unto the end.

Upon Him was laid the iniquity of us all. He, most Meek, was scourged for my anger ; He, most Humble, bore the sentence of my pride ; He, Whose very Name is Love, for my selfishness endured the pains of Death, that through the Cross I might attain to life and immortality.

He emptied Himself, that we might be filled. The hunger and thirst of humanity reaching out to the Unseen, the Incarnation of Thy CHRIST doth replenish with all good things. The world which Thou didst make for Thy Glory He hath redeemed by His Death, and still Thy

Work continueth by the abiding of Thy SPIRIT in the Church.

I praise, I bless, I glorify Thee, O Holy TRINITY, for the Love wherewith Thou hast loved us. Let me shew forth Thy Praise in holiness of life, offering to Thee the Sacrifice of Righteousness, that my heart and mind and strength may render to Thee of Thine Own, and yield the fruits of Grace.

To this end was I born, and for this cause came I into the world, that I might follow the blessed example of Him Who hath said, 'Be ye holy, for I am holy.' Verily it is enough for the disciple that he be as his Master.

Give me grace, O LORD JESU CHRIST, to follow Thee! Thou hast called me to the fellowship of Thy sufferings ;—let me thank Thee for this token of Thy Love. Not in words nor in prayers alone, but in deed and in truth, let me follow in Thy steps and share Thy Crucifixion. Thou didst not spare Thyself ;—let me not spare myself. Give me a generous, a noble, a loving heart, that I may spend it all in loving, and in living for, Thee. Amen.

PSALM IV. Cum invocarem.

HEAR me when I call, O GOD of my righteousness : Thou hast set me at liberty when I was in trouble ; have mercy upon me, and hearken unto my prayer.

O ye sons of men, how long will ye blaspheme Mine honour : and have such pleasure in vanity, and seek after leasing?

Know this also, that the LORD hath chosen to Himself the man that is godly : when I call upon the LORD, He will hear me.

Stand in awe and sin not : commune with your own heart, and in your chamber, and be still.

Offer the sacrifice of righteousness : and put your trust in the LORD.

There be many that say : Who will shew us any good ?

LORD, lift Thou up : the light of Thy countenance upon us.

Thou hast put gladness in my heart : since the time that their corn, and wine, and oil increased.

I will lay me down in peace, and take my rest : for it is Thou, LORD, only, that makest me dwell in safety.

Glory be to the FATHER, and to the SON : and to the HOLY GHOST ;

As it was in the beginning, is now, and ever shall be : world without end. Amen.

Renewal.

He giveth Power to the faint, and to them that have no might He increaseth Strength.

THOU speakest, O my SAVIOUR, unto Thine Own, saying, 'Come unto Me and I will refresh you.'

And the Refreshment which Thou givest is Thyself, the Living Bread from Heaven, the Life of them that believe, and the Resurrection of the dead,—which in the Eucharist Thou dost bestow to sustain our souls.

Here only need we seek that for which our heart panteth,—that which alone satisfieth, alone healeth, alone delighteth ; where Thou dost give Thyself to purge away our stains, to transform our unloveliness, making us like unto Thyself.

Draw me therefore, Blessed LORD, as Thou hast said, unto Thyself. Grant me with the eye of the soul and of faith to behold Thee in the Mystery of Thy Redeeming Love, where at the Altar Thy Saving Passion intercedeth still for man.

There is seen Thy Humility, so marvellous that Angels may not know its wondrous depths ; Thy Obedience, so salutary that it won for us Salvation ; Thy Patience, so long-suffering that it waiteth yet for man ; Thy Meekness, so eloquent that it pleads aloud to the FATHER still ; Thy Purity, so radiant that the Heaven's bright sun before it pales ; Thy Love, so pitiful that still it calls mankind its Own.

There is that most sure word of Thine fulfilled : I, if I be lifted up, will draw all men unto Me. Draw me, O Good JESU, unto Thyself, even me, that I may be healed.

Renew my strength ; console my sorrows ; pardon my sins. Conform me ; transform me ! By Thy Blessed Sacrament, LORD JESU, deliver me and save me. Amen.

PSALM XXIII.   Dominus regit me.

THE LORD is my Shepherd : therefore can I lack nothing.

He shall feed me in a green pasture : and lead me forth beside the waters of comfort.

He shall convert my soul : and bring me forth in the paths of righteousness, for His Name's sake.

Yea, though I walk through the valley of the shadow of death, I will fear no evil :

for Thou art with me ; Thy rod and Thy staff comfort me.

Thou shalt prepare a table before me against them that trouble me : Thou hast anointed my head with oil, and my cup shall be full.

But Thy loving-kindness and mercy shall follow me all the days of my life : and I will dwell in the house of the LORD for ever.

Glory be to the FATHER, and to the SON : and to the HOLY GHOST ;

As it was in the beginning, is now, and ever shall be : world without end. Amen.

Union with God.

Unto Thee, O Lord, will I lift up my soul.

O FATHER of all flesh, Preserver and Lover of the souls of men, Thou that art very high exalted, to Thee, O LORD, do I lift up my soul, longing and fainting for Thee, gasping unto Thee as a thirsty land.

And Thou art the GOD that heareth prayer. The unuttered, inexpressible desire of the soul reacheth unto Thy Heart, and Thine Ear hearkeneth thereto : Thou needest not that we should testify unto Thee, for Thou art He that knoweth all things.

Thou seest me laden with infirmities, weary in the warfare of the spirit against the flesh, bowed down at times with failures, yearning for a nearer conformity to Thy Will, yet still the slave of my own desires ; Thou knowest all of me that I know of myself, and far more.

Yet Thou, O Holy One, dost not despise me. Thou drawest me to Thyself by the cords of a Man, even by the Humanity of Thy SON. He standeth before the Throne of Thy Majesty, uplifting His Pierced Hands, presenting before Thee the Sacrifice of His Incarnation, ever living to make Intercession for us.

Through the Vail, that is to say, His Flesh, we too have access to Thy Presence, and truly our Communion, O FATHER Almighty, is with Thee, through JESUS CHRIST, our LORD.

Teach me the things concerning Thyself. Let me meditate upon them, and give myself wholly to them. Heaven and earth are full of the Majesty of Thy Glory; O let not my soul alone be empty of Thee. Fill Thou my heart with the grace which Thou hast prepared for the sons of men, and lead me in the Way Everlasting.

Bid me seek Thee in all things, that I may find Thee everywhere. Make me to realise that the Word is indeed very near me, in my heart and in my mouth. Give me the blessedness of knowing the very truth of Thy perpetual Presence. Let me own Thee present in sorrow, in sickness, in loneliness of heart,—in whatever Thy Will for me shall be. And so shall I ever dwell with my Lord. Through JESUS CHRIST. Amen.

O Blessed Master, Who hast promised that where Thou art, there shall Thy servant be, I pray Thee by the Mystery of Thy Eucharistic Presence to fulfil Thy gracious word in me, and thus to satisfy the desire of my soul.   Amen.

PSALM CXXXIX.   Domine, probasti.

O LORD, Thou hast searched me out and known me : Thou knowest my down-sitting, and mine up-rising ; Thou understandest my thoughts long before.

Thou art about my path, and about my bed : and spiest out all my ways.

For lo, there is not a word in my tongue : but Thou, O LORD, knowest it altogether.

Thou hast fashioned me behind and before : and laid Thine hand upon me.

Such knowledge is too wonderful and excellent for me : I cannot attain unto it.

Whither shall I go then from Thy SPIRIT : or whither shall I go then from Thy Presence?

If I climb up into heaven, Thou art there : if I go down to hell, Thou art there also.

If I take the wings of the morning : and remain in the uttermost parts of the sea;

Even there also shall Thy hand lead me : and Thy right hand shall hold me.

If I say, Peradventure the darkness shall cover me: then shall my night be turned to day.

Yea, the darkness is no darkness with

Thee, but the night is as clear as the day: the darkness and light to Thee are both alike.

For my reins are Thine : Thou hast covered me in my mother's womb.

I will give thanks unto Thee, for I am fearfully and wonderfully made : marvellous are Thy works, and that my soul knoweth right well.

My bones are not hid from Thee: though I be made secretly, and fashioned beneath in the earth.

Thine eyes did see my substance, yet being imperfect : and in Thy book were all my members written ;

Which day by day were fashioned: when as yet there was none of them.

How dear are Thy counsels unto me, O GOD : O how great is the sum of them !

If I tell them, they are more in number than the sand : when I wake up I am present with Thee.

Wilt Thou not slay the wicked, O GOD: depart from me, ye blood-thirsty men.

For they speak unrighteously against Thee : and Thine enemies take Thy Name in vain.

Do not I hate them, O LORD, that hate Thee : and am not I grieved with those that rise up against Thee ?

Yea, I hate them right sore : even as though they were mine enemies.

Try me, O GOD, and seek the ground of my heart : prove me, and examine my thoughts.

Look well if there be any way of wickedness in me : and lead me in the way everlasting.

Glory be to the FATHER, and to the SON : and to the HOLY GHOST ;

As it was in the beginning, is now, and ever shall be : world without end. Amen.

Sanctification.

Sanctify yourselves, for to-morrow the LORD will do wonders among you.

I WILL wash my hands in innocency, O LORD, and so will I go to Thine Altar.

I said, I will confess my sins unto the LORD, and so Thou forgavest the wickedness of my sin.

For we have an Advocate with the FATHER, JESUS CHRIST, the Righteous, and He is the Propitiation for our sins.

Now are we the sons of GOD, and it doth not yet appear what we shall be ; but we know that when He shall appear we shall be like Him, for we shall see Him as He is.

And every man that hath this hope in Him, purifieth himself.

A PRAYER TO THE HOLY GHOST.

O THOU Love of GOD, Holy Bond of the Almighty FATHER and His Blessed SON, Almighty SPIRIT, the Comforter, Most Merciful Consoler of the sorrowful, come Thou now with Thy Powerful Virtue into the inmost recesses of my heart, and all the dark hiding-places of Thy neglected temple, do Thou, a Loving Indweller, make joyous with the brightness of Thy Light.

I believe that whomsoever Thou sanctifiest Thou makest to be the abode of the FATHER and the SON. Blessed is he in whom Thou dwellest, for by Thee the FATHER and the SON will come and make Their abode with him.

Come then, come, O most benign Comforter of the sorrowful soul in time of need, and Helper in tribulations. Come, Purifier of sins, Healer of wounds, Strength of the frail, Teacher of the humble, Destroyer of the proud ; Come, loving FATHER of the fatherless, Hope of the poor, Restorer of them that are failing. Come, Star of the voyagers, Harbour of the shipwrecked. Come, Thou special Glory of all the living, Only Salvation of the dying. Come, Most HOLY SPIRIT, come and have pity upon me; graciously grant unto me that my littleness may be acceptable to Thy Greatness, my weakness to Thy Strength, according to the multitude of Thy Compassions, which fail not. Amen.

O GOD, Whose Blessed SON was manifested that He might destroy the works of the devil, and make us the sons of GOD and heirs of Eternal Life ; grant, we beseech Thee, that, having this hope, we may purify ourselves, even as He is Pure, that by His Glorious Eucharist below we may be so transformed into the Image of the Heavenly, that we may be like unto Him in His Eternal and Glorious Kingdom ; where with Thee, O FATHER, and Thee, O HOLY GHOST, He liveth and reigneth, ever one GOD, world without end. Amen.

PSALM XXVI. Judica me, Domine.

BE Thou my Judge, O LORD, for I have walked innocently : my trust hath been also in the LORD, therefore shall I not fall.

Examine me, O LORD, and prove me : try out my reins and my heart.

For Thy loving-kindness is ever before mine eyes : and I will walk in Thy truth.

I have not dwelt with vain persons : neither will I have fellowship with the deceitful.

I have hated the congregation of the wicked : and will not sit among the ungodly.

I will wash my hands in innocency, O
LORD : and so will I go to Thine Altar ;

That I may shew the voice of thanksgiving : and tell of all Thy wondrous works.

LORD, I have loved the habitation of
Thy house : and the place where Thine
honour dwelleth.

O shut not up my soul with the sinners:
nor my life with the blood-thirsty;

In whose hands is wickedness: and their
right hand is full of gifts.

But as for me, I will walk innocently:
O deliver me, and be merciful unto me.

My foot standeth right: I will praise the
LORD in the congregations.

Glory be to the FATHER, and to the
SON : and to the HOLY GHOST ;

As it was in the beginning, is now, and
ever shall be : world without end. Amen.

The Approach of Christ.

Thine eyes shall see the King in His beauty.

I HAVE waited for Thee, O LORD, more than they that watch for the morning. I sleep, but my heart waketh. It is the voice of my Beloved that knocketh, saying, Open unto Me.

I lift up mine eyes unto the hills, from whence cometh my Help. High on the mountains of His Eternity He reigneth, Who in the Sacrament of the Altar maketh still His Tabernacle with the sons of men, with whom are His delights.

How happy, how glorious, how holy is that Place of His Rest! with how great eagerness to be sought! the Breath of His Sweetness cometh to me from afar, which is the fragrance of frankincense and myrrh.

How glorious art Thou, O LORD JESU CHRIST! There is no beauty beyond, no comeliness beside, which may compare with Thee, the Fountain of Universal Beauty, the Altogether Lovely.

With joy and gladness let me be

brought, and let me enter into the King's Palace.

Come nigh unto me, LORD; appear to me, and I shall be comforted; shew me Thy Face, and I shall be whole. Feed me with Thyself, that I may live. Let me this day behold the Beauty of my King, and from His Hands receive Himself, Who is our Life, our Joy, our exceeding great Reward.

Inflame me with Thy Presence; transform me into Thy Likeness; let Thy Eucharist be to me this day the comfort of my sorrows and the pledge of future glory.

I come, O LORD, to Thee; I, a sinner, to Thee the SAVIOUR; I, thirsty, to Thee the Fountain of Living Water; I, hungry, to Thee, the Bread of Life. Weary, do Thou give me rest; fainting, do Thou renew my strength; defiled, restore my purity; dying, be Thou my Life!

Even for the rebellious children Thou hast gifts, and him that cometh unto Thee Thou wilt in no wise cast out. Thou art Healing to the sick, Joy to the sorrowful, Peace to the penitent, Glory to those whose faces Thou hast made ashamed; the All in All of those who will have Thee for their own. I have nothing, but do Thou supply my need. Give what Thou commandest, and command what Thou wilt.

Despise not my unworthiness, but behold my want. Disdain not my poverty, but consider my desire. Turn not Thou Thy Face away from me, but look upon my tears. Accept my obedience unto Thee, my King, this day. Amen.

May the very GOD of peace sanctify me wholly; and I pray GOD that my whole spirit and soul and body be preserved blameless unto the coming of the LORD JESUS. Amen.

PSALM XLV. Eructabit cor meum.

MY heart is inditing of a good matter: I speak of the things which I have made unto the King.

My tongue is the pen : of a ready writer.

Thou art fairer than the children of men : full of grace are Thy lips, because GOD hath blessed Thee for ever.

Gird Thee with Thy sword upon Thy thigh, O Thou most Mighty : according to Thy worship and renown.

Good luck have Thou with Thine honour: ride on, because of the word of truth, of meekness, and righteousness ; and Thy right hand shall teach Thee terrible things.

Thy arrows are very sharp, and the people shall be subdued unto Thee : even in the midst among the King's enemies.

Thy seat, O GOD, endureth for ever : the sceptre of Thy kingdom is a right sceptre.

Thou hast loved righteousness, and

hated iniquity : wherefore GOD, even Thy
GOD, hath anointed Thee with the oil of
gladness above Thy fellows.

All Thy garments smell of myrrh, aloes,
and cassia : out of the ivory palaces,
whereby they have made Thee glad.

Kings' daughters were among Thy
honourable women : upon Thy right hand
did stand the queen in a vesture of gold,
wrought about with divers colours.

Hearken, O daughter, and consider,
incline thine ear : forget also thine own
people, and thy father's house.

So shall the King have pleasure in thy
beauty : for He is thy LORD GOD, and
worship thou Him.

And the daughter of Tyre shall be there
with a gift : like as the rich also among
the people shall make their supplication
before thee.

The King's daughter is all glorious
within : her clothing is of wrought gold.

She shall be brought unto the King in
raiment of needle-work : the virgins that
be her fellows shall bear her company,
and shall be brought unto thee.

With joy and gladness shall they be
brought : and shall enter into the King's
palace.

Instead of thy fathers thou shalt have
children : whom thou mayest make
princes in all lands.

I will remember Thy Name from one generation to another : therefore shall the people give thanks unto Thee, world without end.

Glory be to the FATHER, and to the SON : and to the HOLY GHOST ;
As it was in the beginning, is now, and ever shall be : world without end. Amen.

The Divine Guest.

To-day I must abide at thy house.

O GOD, the FATHER of our LORD JESUS CHRIST, the FATHER of Mercies and of sinful men, have mercy upon me, and save me. Forgive me all my sin, and give me what Thou knowest that I need. Remove far from me all pride, uncleanness, and self-will, and fill me instead with faith, purity, and obedience, that in all things I may please Thee. Give me, if Thou wilt, a loving penitence, and a true humility, that where sin hath abounded grace may much more abound.

And grant that by this Holy Communion I may find the remission of my sins, the quieting of my conscience, the sanctification and salvation of my soul; to the glory of Thy Name, through JESUS CHRIST our LORD. Amen.

LORD, I am not worthy that Thou shouldest come under my roof: but speak the word only, and Thy servant shall be healed. LORD, if Thou wilt, Thou canst make me clean! So cleanse me that

Thou mayest enter in and abide with me for ever. Amen.

PSALM XV. Domine, quis habitabit?

LORD, who shall dwell in Thy tabernacle : or who shall rest upon Thy holy hill?

Even he, that leadeth an uncorrupt life : and doeth the thing which is right, and speaketh the truth from his heart.

He that hath used no deceit in his tongue, nor done evil to his neighbour : and hath not slandered his neighbour.

He that setteth not by himself, but is lowly in his own eyes : and maketh much of them that fear the LORD.

He that sweareth unto his neighbour, and disappointeth him not : though it were to his own hindrance.

He that hath not given his money upon usury : nor taken reward against the innocent.

Whoso doeth these things : shall never fall.

Glory be to the FATHER, and to the SON : and to the HOLY GHOST ;

As it was in the beginning, is now, and ever shall be : world without end. Amen.

The Order of the Administration of the Holy Communion, with Devotions for Use during the Celebration.

It is I Myself, handle Me and see.

NOTE.

'*So many as intend to be partakers of the Holy Communion shall signify their names to the Curate, at least some time the day before.*'

'*And because it is requisite, that no man should come to the Holy Communion, but with a full trust in GOD'S mercy, and with a quiet conscience; therefore if there be any who cannot quiet his own conscience, but requireth further comfort or counsel, let him come to some discreet and learned minister of GOD'S Word, and open his grief; that by the ministry of GOD'S Holy Word he may receive the benefit of Absolution.*'

From the BOOK OF COMMON PRAYER.

At the Divine Office.

Before the Service begins.

IN the Name of the ✠ FATHER, and of the SON, and of the HOLY GHOST. Amen.

Ant. I will go unto the Altar of GOD.

PSALM XLIII. Judica me, Deus.

GIVE sentence with me, O GOD, and defend my cause against the ungodly people : O deliver me from the deceitful and wicked man.

For Thou art the GOD of my strength, why hast Thou put me from Thee : and why go I so heavily, while the enemy oppresseth me?

O send out Thy light and Thy truth, that they may lead me : and bring me unto Thy holy hill, and to Thy dwelling.

And that I may go unto the altar of GOD, even unto the GOD of my joy and gladness : and upon the harp will I give thanks unto Thee, O GOD, my GOD.

Why art thou so heavy, O my soul : and why art thou so disquieted within me?

O put thy trust in GOD : for I will yet give Him thanks, Which is the help of my countenance, and my GOD.

Glory be to the FATHER, and to the SON : and to the HOLY GHOST ;

As it was in the beginning, is now, and ever shall be : world without end. Amen.

Ant. I will go unto the Altar of GOD, even unto the GOD of my joy and gladness.

I CONFESS to Almighty GOD, that I have sinned exceedingly in thought, word, and deed, through my own grievous fault ; wherefore I pray Almighty GOD to have mercy upon me, to forgive me my sins, and to deliver me from every evil ; to confirm and strengthen me in goodness, and to bring me to everlasting life. Amen.

In the spirit of humility, and with a contrite heart, let us be accepted of Thee, O LORD ; and let our Sacrifice be in such wise in Thy sight, that it may be accepted of Thee this day, and please Thee, O LORD my GOD.

We purpose to offer to Thee, as is our bounden duty, this holy and spotless Sacrifice, in adoration of Thy Majesty, and as a Memorial of the Precious Death of Thy dear SON, CHRIST our LORD, in thanksgiving for the graces and blessings which Thou bestowest on Thy Church, and for the obtaining of all needful things both for ourselves and for all those for whom we desire to pray; for the sanctification of the living, and the repose of the dead; and also [*Here name any special intention*].

At the Introit.

JESUS CHRIST the Sacrifice for sin, the Priest for ever, after the order of Melchisedec, standeth in the Holy of Holies, and maketh reconciliation for the people.

When the Priest prays before the Altar.

IF thou hadst the purity of an angel, and the sanctity of S. John Baptist, thou couldest not be worthy either to receive or to handle this Sacrament.

Let Thy Priests, O LORD, be clothed with righteousness, especially he who now stands before Thine Altar ministering to us in Thy Holy Things.

And grant, O LORD, that we may

boldly and without blame, with a pure heart and a contrite mind, without shame and confusion, and with sanctified lips, presume to call upon Thee, our GOD and Heavenly FATHER, and say,

OUR FATHER, Which art in heaven, Hallowed be Thy Name. Thy kingdom come. Thy will be done in earth, As it is in heaven. Give us this day our daily bread. And forgive us our trespasses, As we forgive them that trespass against us. And lead us not into temptation ; But deliver us from evil. Amen.

The Collect.

ALMIGHTY GOD, unto Whom all hearts be open, all desires known, and from Whom no secrets are hid ; Cleanse the thoughts of our hearts by the inspiration of Thy HOLY SPIRIT, that we may perfectly love Thee, and worthily magnify Thy holy Name ; through CHRIST our LORD. *Amen.*

¶ *Then shall the Priest, turning to the people, rehearse distinctly all the TEN COMMANDMENTS; and the people still kneeling shall, after every Commandment, ask GOD mercy for their transgression thereof for the time past, and grace to keep the same for the time to come, as followeth.*

Minister.

GOD spake these words, and said; I am the LORD thy GOD: Thou shalt have none other gods but Me.

People. LORD, have mercy upon us, and incline our hearts to keep this law.

Minister. Thou shalt not make to thyself any graven image, nor the likeness of any thing that is in heaven above, or in the earth beneath, or in the water under the earth. Thou shalt not bow down to them, nor worship them: for I the LORD thy GOD am a jealous GOD, and visit the sins of the fathers upon the children, unto the third and fourth generation of them that hate Me, and shew mercy unto thousands in them that love Me, and keep My commandments.

People. LORD, have mercy upon us, and incline our hearts to keep this law.

Minister. Thou shalt not take the Name of the LORD thy GOD in vain: for the LORD will not hold him guiltless that taketh His Name in vain.

People. LORD, have mercy upon us, and incline our hearts to keep this law.

Minister. Remember that thou keep holy the Sabbath-day. Six days shalt thou labour, and do all that thou hast to do; but the seventh day is the Sabbath of the LORD thy GOD. In it thou shalt do no manner of work, thou, and thy son, and thy daughter, thy man-servant, and thy maid-servant, thy cattle, and the stranger that is within thy gates. For in six days the LORD made heaven and earth, the sea, and all that in them is, and rested the seventh day : wherefore the LORD blessed the seventh day, and hallowed it.

People. LORD, have mercy upon us, and incline our hearts to keep this law.

Minister. Honour thy father and thy mother ; that thy days may be long in the land, which the LORD thy GOD giveth thee.

People. LORD, have mercy upon us, and incline our hearts to keep this law.

Minister. Thou shalt do no murder.

People. LORD, have mercy upon us, and incline our hearts to keep this law.

Minister. Thou shalt not commit adultery.

People. LORD, have mercy upon us, and incline our hearts to keep this law.

Minister. Thou shalt not steal.

People. LORD, have mercy upon us, and incline our hearts to keep this law.

Minister. Thou shalt not bear false witness against thy neighbour.

People. LORD, have mercy upon us, and incline our hearts to keep this law.

Minister. Thou shalt not covet thy neighbour's house, thou shalt not covet thy neighbour's wife, nor his servant, nor his maid, nor his ox, nor his ass, nor any thing that is his.

People. LORD, have mercy upon us, and write all these Thy laws in our hearts, we beseech Thee.

¶ *Then shall follow one of these two Collects for the Queen, the Priest standing as before, and saying,*

Let us pray.

ALMIGHTY GOD, Whose kingdom is ever-lasting, and power infinite; Have mercy upon the whole Church; and so rule the heart of Thy chosen Servant, *VICTORIA*, our Queen and Governour, that she (knowing Whose minister she is) may above all things seek Thy honour and glory: and that we, and all her subjects (duly considering Whose authority she hath) may faithfully serve, honour, and humbly obey her, in Thee, and for Thee, according to Thy blessed Word and ordinance; through JESUS CHRIST our LORD, Who with Thee and the HOLY GHOST liveth and reigneth, ever one GOD, world without end. *Amen.*

Or,

ALMIGHTY and everlasting GOD, we are taught by Thy holy Word, that the hearts of Kings are in Thy rule and governance, and that Thou dost dispose and turn them as it seemeth best to Thy godly wisdom: We humbly beseech Thee so to dispose and govern the heart of *VICTORIA* Thy Servant, our Queen and Governour, that, in all her thoughts, words, and works, she may ever seek Thy honour and glory, and study to preserve Thy people committed to her charge, in wealth, peace, and godliness : Grant this, O merciful FATHER, for Thy dear SON's sake, JESUS CHRIST our LORD. *Amen.*

The Collect.

The Epistle.

Before the Holy Gospel, say,

Glory be to Thee, O LORD.

The Holy Gospel.

The Creed.

I BELIEVE in one GOD the FATHER Almighty, Maker of heaven and earth, And of all things visible and invisible :

And in one LORD JESUS CHRIST, the only-begotten SON of GOD, Begotten of His FATHER before all worlds, GOD of GOD, Light of Light, Very GOD of very GOD, Begotten, not made, Being of one substance with the FATHER ; By Whom all things were made : Who for us men, and for our salvation came down from heaven, AND WAS INCARNATE BY THE HOLY GHOST OF THE VIRGIN MARY, AND WAS MADE MAN, And was crucified also for us under Pontius Pilate. He suffered and was buried, And the third day He rose again according to the Scriptures, And ascended into heaven, And sitteth on the right hand of the FATHER. And He shall come again with glory to judge both the quick and the dead : Whose kingdom shall have no end.

And I believe in the HOLY GHOST, the LORD and Giver of life, Who proceedeth from the FATHER and the SON, Who with the FATHER and the SON together is worshipped and glorified, Who spake by the Prophets.   And I believe one Catholick and Apostolick Church.   I acknowledge one Baptism for the remission of sins, And I look for the Resurrection of the dead, And the life of the world to come.   Amen.

The Offertory.

LET your light so shine before men, that they may see your good works, and glorify your FATHER Which is in heaven.

During the preparation of the Oblations you may say the following Devotions.

O GOD, Who hast prepared for them that love Thee such good things as pass man's understanding ; Pour into our hearts such love toward Thee, that we, loving Thee above all things, may obtain Thy promises, which exceed all that we can desire ; through JESUS CHRIST our LORD.   Amen.

Govern, we beseech Thee, O LORD, Thy servant our Bishop, and multiply upon him the gifts of Thy Grace, that he, being guided by Thy HOLY SPIRIT, may in all things fulfil Thy perfect will, and may rejoice in never-failing benediction ; through JESUS CHRIST our LORD.   Amen.

May it please Thee, O LORD, to bless our persecutors, to grant them true repentance, and to guide their feet into the way of peace.   Amen.

Absolve, we beseech Thee, O LORD, the souls of Thy servants departed this life in Thy faith and fear. . . . And whatsoever they have done amiss in their human conversation through the frailty of the flesh, do Thou cleanse away by the pardon of Thy most merciful loving-kindness in JESUS CHRIST our LORD.   Amen.

Receive, we beseech Thee, the prayers of Thy people which call upon Thee. Hear Thou in Heaven, Thy Dwelling-place, and when Thou hearest, forgive.

The Priest shall say,

Let us pray for the whole state of CHRIST'S Church militant here in earth.

ALMIGHTY and everliving GOD, Who by Thy holy Apostle hast taught us to make prayers, and supplications, and to give thanks, or all men ;

We humbly beseech Thee most mercifully to accept our alms and oblations, and to receive these our prayers, which we offer unto Thy Divine Majesty;

Beseeching Thee to inspire continually the universal Church with the spirit of truth, unity, and concord : And grant, that all they that do confess Thy holy Name may agree in the truth of Thy holy Word, and live in unity, and godly love.

We beseech Thee also to save and defend all Christian Kings, Princes, and Governours ; and specially Thy servant *VICTORIA* our Queen ; that under her we may be godly and quietly governed : And grant unto her whole Council, and to all that are put in authority under her, that they may truly and indifferently minister justice, to the punishment of wickedness and vice, and to the maintenance of Thy true religion, and virtue.

Give grace, O heavenly FATHER, to all Bishops and Curates, that they may both by their life and doctrine set forth Thy true and lively Word, and rightly and duly administer Thy holy Sacraments :

And to all Thy people give Thy heavenly grace ; and especially to this congregation here present ; that, with meek heart and due reverence, they may hear, and receive Thy holy Word ; truly serving Thee in holiness and righteousness all the days of their life.

And we most humbly beseech Thee of Thy goodness, O LORD, to comfort and succour all them, who in this transitory life are in trouble, sorrow, need, sickness, or any other adversity.

And we also bless Thy holy Name for all Thy

servants departed this life in Thy faith and fear ; beseeching Thee to give us grace so to follow their good examples, that with them we may be partakers of Thy heavenly kingdom : Grant this, O FATHER, for JESUS CHRIST'S sake, our only Mediator and Advocate. *Amen.*

After the Prayer for the Church.

TO Thee do I look up ; in Thee do I trust, my GOD, FATHER of Mercies. Bless and sanctify my soul with heavenly blessing, that it may become Thy holy habitation, and the seat of Thy Eternal Glory ; and let nothing be found, where Thou deignest to dwell, that may offend the eyes of Thy Majesty.

The Exhortation.

Then shall the Priest say to them that come to receive the Holy Communion,

YE that do truly and earnestly repent you of your sins, and are in love and charity with your neighbours, and intend to lead a new life, following the commandments of GOD, and walking from henceforth in His holy ways ; Draw near with faith, and take this Holy Sacrament to your comfort ; and make your humble confession to Almighty GOD, meekly kneeling upon your knees.

The Confession.

ALMIGHTY GOD, FATHER of our LORD JESUS CHRIST, Maker of all things, Judge of all men ; We acknowledge and bewail our manifold sins and wickedness, Which we, from time to time, most grievously have committed, By thought, word, and deed, Against Thy Divine Majesty, Provoking most justly Thy wrath and indignation against us. We do earnestly repent, And are heartily sorry for these our misdoings : The remembrance of them is grievous unto us ; The burden of them is intolerable. Have mercy upon us, Have mercy upon us, most merciful FATHER ; For Thy SON our LORD JESUS CHRIST'S sake, Forgive us all that is past ; And grant that we may ever hereafter Serve and please thee In newness of life, To the honour and glory of Thy Name ; Through JESUS CHRIST our LORD. Amen.

The Absolution.

ALMIGHTY GOD, our heavenly FATHER, Who of His great mercy hath promised forgiveness of sins to all them that with hearty repentance and true faith turn unto Him ; Have mercy upon you, .pardon and deliver you from all your sins, confirm and strengthen you in all goodness, and bring you to everlasting life : through JESUS CHRIST our LORD. *Amen.*

The Comfortable Words.

Hear what comfortable words our SAVIOUR CHRIST saith unto all that truly turn to Him.

COME unto Me all that travail and are heavy laden, and I will refresh you.

S. Matth. xi. 28.

So GOD loved the world, that He gave His only-begotten SON, to the end that all that believe in Him should not perish, but have everlasting life. S. John iii. 16.

Hear also what Saint Paul saith.

This is a true saying, and worthy of all men to be received, That CHRIST JESUS came into the world to save sinners. 1 Tim. i. 15.

Hear also what Saint John saith.

If any man sin, we have an Advocate with the FATHER, JESUS CHRIST the righteous ; and He is the Propitiation for our sins. 1 S. John ii. 1.

Sursum Corda.

Priest. Lift up your hearts.
Answer. We lift them up unto the LORD.
Priest. Let us give thanks unto our LORD GOD.
Answer. It is meet and right so to do.

Preface.

IT is very meet, right, and our bounden duty, that we should at all times, and in all places, give thanks unto Thee, O LORD, *Holy FATHER, Almighty, Everlasting GOD.

These words [Holy FATHER] must be omitted on Trinity Sunday.

¶ *Here shall follow the Proper Preface, according to the time, if there be any specially appointed: or else immediately shall follow,*

THEREFORE with Angels and Archangels, and with all the company of heaven, we laud and magnify Thy glorious Name ; evermore praising Thee, and saying :

Sanctus.

Holy, Holy, Holy, LORD GOD of Hosts, heaven and earth are full of Thy glory : Glory be to Thee, O LORD most High. *Amen.*

PROPER PREFACES.

Upon Christmas Day, *and seven days after.*

BECAUSE Thou didst give JESUS CHRIST Thine only SON to be born as at this time for us ; Who, by the operation of the HOLY GHOST, was made very Man of the substance of the Virgin Mary His Mother ; and that without spot of sin, to make us clean from all sin. Therefore with Angels, &c.

Upon Easter Day, *and seven days after.*

BUT chiefly are we bound to praise Thee for the glorious Resurrection of Thy SON JESUS CHRIST our LORD : for He is the very Paschal Lamb, Which was offered for us, and hath taken away the sin of the world ; Who by His Death hath destroyed death, and by His Rising to life again hath restored to us everlasting life.   Therefore with Angels, *&c.*

Upon Ascension Day, *and seven days after.*

THROUGH Thy most dearly beloved SON JESUS CHRIST our LORD ; Who after His most glorious Resurrection manifestly appeared to all His Apostles, and in their sight Ascended up into Heaven to prepare a place for us ; that where He is, thither we might also ascend, and reign with Him in glory.   Therefore with Angels, *&c.*

Upon Whitsun Day, *and six days after.*

THROUGH JESUS CHRIST our LORD ; according to Whose most true promise, the HOLY GHOST came down as at this time from heaven with a sudden great sound, as it had been a mighty wind, in the likeness of fiery tongues, lighting upon the Apostles, to teach them, and to lead them to all truth ; giving them both the gift of divers languages, and also boldness with fervent zeal constantly to preach the Gospel unto all nations ; whereby we have been brought out of darkness and error into the clear light and true knowledge of Thee, and of Thy SON JESUS CHRIST.   Therefore with Angels, &c.

Upon the Feast of Trinity *only.*

WHO art One GOD, One LORD ; not One only Person, but Three Persons in One Substance.   For that which we believe of the glory of the FATHER, the same we believe of the SON, and of the HOLY GHOST, without any difference or inequality.   Therefore with Angels, &c.

In the pause which generally occurs in this place, you may pray thus :

DRAW near, O LORD JESUS CHRIST our GOD, from the habitation of Thy dwelling and Throne of Glory in Thy Kingdom, and come and sanctify us. O Thou, Who sittest on high at the Right Hand of the FATHER, and at the same time art verily present with us below, vouchsafe to impart to us by Thy Mighty Hand Thy Sacred Body and Thy most Precious Blood.

The Prayer of Humble Access.

WE do not presume to come to this Thy Table, O merciful LORD, trusting in our own righteousness, but in Thy manifold and great mercies.   We are not worthy so much as to gather up the crumbs under Thy Table.   But Thou art the same LORD, Whose property is always to have mercy : Grant us therefore, gracious LORD, so to eat the Flesh of Thy dear SON JESUS CHRIST, and to drink His Blood, that our sinful bodies may be made clean by His Body, and our souls washed through His most Precious Blood, and that we may evermore dwell in Him, and He in us.   *Amen.*

Prepare to meet your GOD, and say privately,

COME, O Almighty and Eternal GOD, the Sanctifier, and bless this Sacrifice prepared for the Glory of Thy holy Name.

Grant, O LORD, that this Holy Communion may be, to all who shall partake of It, for the remission of sins, and for the sanctification of soul and body unto Everlasting Life.   Amen.

Blessed is He that cometh in the Name of the LORD ; Hosanna in the Highest.

The Canon.

ALMIGHTY GOD, our heavenly FATHER, Who of Thy tender mercy didst give Thine only SON JESUS CHRIST to suffer Death upon the Cross for our Redemption ; Who made there (by His one Oblation of Himself once offered) a full, perfect, and sufficient Sacrifice, Oblation, and Satisfaction, for the sins of the whole world ; and did institute, and in His holy Gospel command us to continue, a perpetual memory of that His precious Death until His Coming again ;

Hear us, O merciful FATHER, we most humbly beseech Thee ; and grant that we receiving these Thy creatures of Bread and Wine, according to Thy SON our SAVIOUR JESUS CHRIST'S holy Institution, in remembrance of His Death and Passion, may be partakers of His most Blessed Body and Blood :

Who, in the same night that He was betrayed, took Bread ; and when He had given thanks, He brake It, and gave It to His dis- *Consecration of* ciples, saying, Take, eat, 𝕿𝖍𝖎𝖘 𝖎𝖘 *the Bread.* 𝕸𝖞 𝕭𝖔𝖉𝖞 𝖜𝖍𝖎𝖈𝖍 𝖎𝖘 𝖌𝖎𝖛𝖊𝖓 𝖋𝖔𝖗 𝖞𝖔𝖚: Do this in remembrance of Me.

Likewise after Supper He took the Cup ; and, when He had given thanks, He gave It to them, saying, Drink ye all of this ; 𝖋𝖔𝖗 𝕿𝖍𝖎𝖘 𝖎𝖘 𝕸𝖞 𝕭𝖑𝖔𝖔𝖉 𝖔𝖋 𝖙𝖍𝖊 𝕹𝖊𝖜 𝕿𝖊𝖘𝖙𝖆𝖒𝖊𝖓𝖙, 𝖜𝖍𝖎𝖈𝖍 𝖎𝖘 *Consecration* 𝖘𝖍𝖊𝖉 𝖋𝖔𝖗 𝖞𝖔𝖚 𝖆𝖓𝖉 𝖋𝖔𝖗 𝖒𝖆𝖓𝖞 𝖋𝖔𝖗 𝖙𝖍𝖊 𝕽𝖊= *of the Cup.* 𝖒𝖎𝖘𝖘𝖎𝖔𝖓 𝖔𝖋 𝕾𝖎𝖓𝖘: Do this, as oft as ye shall drink It, in remembrance of Me. *Amen.*

At the Consecration of the Elements, say,

' L O ! this is our GOD, we have waited for Him, and He will save us ; This is the LORD, we have waited for Him ; we will be glad and rejoice in His Salvation.'

During the pause which follows the solemn Act of Consecration, adore and worship your present GOD.

I BEHELD, and lo, in the midst of the Throne stood a LAMB as It had been slain. And I heard the voice of many Angels round about the Throne saying, with a loud voice, Worthy is the LAMB that was slain to receive power, and riches, and wisdom, and strength, and honour, and glory and blessing.

O LAMB of GOD, that takest away the sins of the world,
>Have mercy upon us !

O LAMB of GOD, that takest away the sins of the world,
>Have mercy upon us !

O LAMB of GOD, that takest away the sins of the world,
>Grant us Thy Peace !

At the Communion of the Priest.

MAY the Body and Blood of our LORD JESUS CHRIST preserve thy body and soul unto Everlasting Life. Amen.

The LORD grant thee thy heart's desire, and fulfil all thy mind. The LORD, the Righteous Judge, reward thee at the Last Day with the Crown of righteousness prepared for all them that love His appearing.

ACTS OF ADORATION.

I.

THEE we adore, O hidden SAVIOUR, Thee,
Who in Thy Sacrament dost deign to be :
Both flesh and spirit at Thy Presence fail,
Yet here Thy Presence we devoutly hail.

O blest Memorial of our dying LORD,
Who living Bread to men doth here afford !
O may our souls for ever feed on Thee,
And Thou, O CHRIST, for ever precious be.

Fountain of goodness, JESU, LORD and GOD,
Cleanse us, unclean, with Thy most cleansing Blood ;
Increase our faith and love, that we may know
The hope and peace which from Thy Presence flow.

O CHRIST, Whom now beneath a veil we see,
May what we thirst for soon our portion be,
To gaze on Thee unveiled, and see Thy Face,
The vision of Thy glory and Thy grace.
Amen.

II.

BEHOLD the LAMB of GOD !
       O Thou for sinners slain,
Let it not be in vain
       That Thou hast died :
Thee for my SAVIOUR let me take,
My only refuge let me make
       Thy Piercèd Side.

   Behold the LAMB of GOD !
Into the sacred flood
Of Thy most Precious Blood
       My soul I cast :
Wash me and make me clean within,
And keep me pure from every sin,
       Till life be past.

   Behold the LAMB of GOD !
All hail, Incarnate WORD,
Thou Everlasting LORD,
       SAVIOUR most Blest ;
Fill us with love that never faints,
Grant us with all Thy blessed Saints
       Eternal Rest.

   Behold the LAMB of GOD !
Worthy is He alone
To sit upon the Throne
       Of GOD above ;
One with the Ancient of all Days,
One with the COMFORTER in praise,
       All light and love.   Amen.

Meditate upon these words of CHRIST.

FATHER, the hour is come; glorify Thy SON, that Thy SON also may glorify Thee.

Thou hast given Him power over all flesh, that He should give Eternal Life to as many as Thou hast given Him.

And this is Life Eternal, that they might know Thee, the only true GOD, and JESUS CHRIST Whom Thou hast sent.

I have manifested Thy Name unto the men which Thou gavest me out of the world. For I have given unto them the words which Thou gavest Me.

Now they have known that all things whatsoever Thou hast given Me are of Thee.

And all Mine are Thine, and Thine are Mine; and I am glorified in them.

And the glory which Thou gavest Me, I have given them; that they may be one, even as We are One.

If you are going to Communicate,
say this Prayer.

O LORD, all things are Thine which are in heaven and in earth. I desire to give myself to Thee as a free-will offering, and to remain Thine for ever.

O LORD, in the simplicity of my heart, I offer myself to Thee to-day, to be Thy servant for ever, to obey Thee, and to be a sacrifice of perpetual praise.

Receive me together with this Holy Oblation of Thy SON'S most Precious Body and Blood, which we offer to Thee this day in the presence of the Angels invisibly assisting ; that It may be for the Salvation both of myself and of all Thy people.

Pardon, O LORD, I beseech Thee, all the sins and offences which I have committed before Thee and Thy holy Angels, from the day in which I first could sin even to this hour ; consume them and burn them with the fire of Thy Love, and blot out all the stains of my sins, and purify my conscience from every fault. Restore to me the Grace which I have lost, clothe me with the garment of Thy Righteousness, and receive me mercifully to the kiss of Peace.

Hear me graciously, I beseech Thee, when I kneel before Thee, my GOD.

Forgive me, O GOD, forgive me my sins, for the sake of Thy holy Name.

Save my soul, which Thou hast redeemed with Thy SON'S most Precious Blood.

As you go up to the Altar, reflect upon these words.

WE have an Altar, and have boldness to enter into the Holiest by the Blood of JESUS, by a New and Living Way which He hath consecrated for us through His Flesh.

JESUS Himself stood in the midst, and saith unto them,

'Peace be unto you.'
'Behold Me that it is I Myself, handle Me and see.'
'He that seeth Me, seeth Him that sent Me.'
'If ye shall ask anything in My Name, I will do it.'
'Not as the world giveth give I unto you.'

Say in your heart as you kneel at the Altar.

LORD, I am not worthy that Thou shouldest come under my roof : but speak the word only, and my soul shall be healed.

As the Priest approaches you with the Blessed Sacrament, say,

WHENCE is this to me that my LORD should come to me ?

Then offer your Intention thus,

TO Thee, O FATHER, do I offer this
Sacrifice of the Body and Blood of
Thy dear SON, in thanksgiving for all
Thy mercies . . . in satisfaction for all
my sins . . . and in humble prayer that
Thou wouldest grant me for His sake
that . . .

The Communion of the Body of Christ.

THE Body of our LORD JESUS CHRIST, which
was given for thee, preserve thy body and
soul unto everlasting life.   Take and eat This in
remembrance that CHRIST died for thee, and
feed on Him in thy heart by faith with thanksgiving.

*As you receive the Blessed Body of your
LORD, welcome Him into your heart
with the greatest possible reverence
and devotion, and say,*

'My LORD and my GOD !'

The Communion of the Blood of Christ.

THE Blood of our LORD JESUS CHRIST, which
was shed for thee, preserve thy body and
soul unto everlasting life.   Drink This in remembrance that CHRIST's Blood was shed for thee,
and be thankful.

*And when you receive His Precious
Blood, say agàin,*

'My LORD and my GOD !'

[*If you are not going to Communicate you
may make the following*

ACT OF SPIRITUAL COMMUNION.

IN union, O LORD, with the faithful at
every Altar where Thy Blessed Body
and Blood are now being presented to
the Eternal FATHER, I venerate these
Holy Mysteries, and since I cannot now
receive Thee sacramentally, I beseech
Thee to enter spiritually into my soul.

Send me not away fasting, lest I faint
by the way.]

THANKSGIVING.

PSALM CIII.   Benedic, anima mea.

PRAISE the LORD, O my soul : and
all that is within me praise His holy
Name.

Praise the LORD, O my soul : and forget not all His benefits ;

Who forgiveth all thy sin : and healeth
all thine infirmities ;

Who saveth thy life from destruction :
and crowneth thee with mercy and loving-
kindness ;

Who satisfieth thy mouth with good things : making thee young and lusty as an eagle.

The LORD executeth righteousness and judgment : for all them that are oppressed with wrong.

He shewed His ways unto Moses : His works unto the children of Israel.

The LORD is full of compassion and mercy : long-suffering, and of great goodness.

He will not alway be chiding : neither keepeth He His anger for ever.

He hath not dealt with us after our sins : nor rewarded us according to our wickednesses.

For look how high the heaven is in comparison of the earth : so great is His mercy also toward them that fear Him.

Look how wide also the east is from the west : so far hath He set our sins from us.

Yea, like as a father pitieth his own children : even so is the LORD merciful unto them that fear Him.

For He knoweth whereof we are made : He remembereth that we are but dust.

The days of man are but as grass : for he flourisheth as a flower of the field.

For as soon as the wind goeth over it, it is gone : and the place thereof shall know it no more.

But the merciful goodness of the LORD endureth for ever and ever upon them that fear Him : and His righteousness upon children's children ;

Even upon such as keep His covenant : and think upon His commandments to do them.

The LORD hath prepared His seat in heaven : and His Kingdom ruleth over all.

O praise the LORD, ye angels of His, ye that excel in strength : ye that fulfil His commandment, and hearken unto the voice of His words.

O praise the LORD, all ye His hosts : ye servants of His that do His pleasure.

O speak good of the LORD, all ye works of His, in all places of His dominion : praise thou the Lord, O my soul.

Glory be to the FATHER, and to the SON : and to the HOLY GHOST ;

As it was in the beginning, is now, and ever shall be : world without end. Amen.

PSALM XCI. Qui habitat.

WHOSO dwelleth under the defence of the Most High : shall abide under the shadow of the Almighty.

I will say unto the LORD, Thou art my Hope, and my Stronghold : my GOD, in Him will I trust.

For He shall deliver thee from the snare of the hunter : and from the noisome pestilence.

He shall defend thee under His wings, and thou shalt be safe under His feathers : His faithfulness and truth shall be thy shield and buckler.

Thou shalt not be afraid for any terror by night : nor for the arrow that flieth by day ;

For the pestilence that walketh in darkness : nor for the sickness that destroyeth in the noon-day.

A thousand shall fall beside thee, and ten thousand at thy right hand : but it shall not come nigh thee.

Yea, with thine eyes shalt thou behold : and see the reward of the ungodly.

For Thou, LORD, art my Hope : Thou hast set Thine house of defence very high.

There shall no evil happen unto thee : neither shall any plague come nigh thy dwelling.

For He shall give His angels charge over thee : to keep thee in all thy ways.

They shall bear thee in their hands : that thou hurt not thy foot against a stone.

Thou shalt go upon the lion and adder : the young lion and the dragon shalt thou tread under thy feet.

Because he hath set his love upon Me, therefore will I deliver him : I will set him up, because he hath known My Name.

He shall call upon Me, and I will hear him : yea, I am with him in trouble ; I will deliver him; and bring him to honour.

With long life will I satisfy him : and shew him My salvation.

Glory be to the FATHER, and to the SON : and to the HOLY GHOST ;

As it was in the beginning, is now, and ever shall be : world without end. Amen.

Magnificat.

M Y soul doth magnify the LORD : and my spirit hath rejoiced in GOD my Saviour.

For He hath regarded : the lowliness of His handmaiden.

For behold, from henceforth : all generations shall call me blessed.

For He that is mighty hath magnified me : and holy is His Name.

And His mercy is on them that fear Him : throughout all generations.

He hath shewed strength with His arm : He hath scattered the proud in the imagination of their hearts.

He hath put down the mighty from their seat : and hath exalted the humble and meek.

He hath filled the hungry with good

things : and the rich He hath sent empty away.

He remembering His mercy hath holpen His servant Israel : as He promised to our forefathers, Abraham and his seed, for ever.

Glory be to the FATHER, and to the SON : and to the HOLY GHOST ;

As it was in the beginning, is now, and ever shall be : world without end. Amen.

O MY GOD and my LORD, my Hope and the Joy of my heart, Thou hast commanded us by Thy SON, saying, 'Ask, and ye shall receive, that your joy may be full.'

But what shall I ask of Thee more than I have already? For here at Thine Altar I have found a joy full, yea, more than full. The SON of Thy Love hath bidden me enter into the joy of my LORD, and that joy hath entered into me and made me glad.

Yet the good things which Thou hast prepared for us in the world to come, eye hath not seen, nor ear heard, neither hath it entered the heart of man to conceive in this life. Here, we do but see in part ; there, face to face we shall behold, and shall know even as also we are known.

Then, too, we shall be like CHRIST, for

we shall see Him as He is. No longer, then, hidden beneath Sacramental veils shall we adore Him, but He will perfectly manifest Himself to us, and sweetly reveal all mysteries to His faithful people.

Until that Day break, and the shadows flee away, I will get me to the mountain of myrrh and the hill of frankincense, the High Altar where the Church uplifts the Memorial of her SAVIOUR'S Death, until He come again.

Here let me day by day hold converse with my LORD, till I be transformed into His Likeness Who, being the Brightness of the FATHER'S Glory, and the express Image of His Person, is Fairest too of all the sons of men.

I pray Thee, O my LORD, that I may know Thee, love Thee, rejoice in Thee; and though I cannot fully, in this life, yet let me at least, by the virtue of Thy Blessed Sacrament, advance daily, until that which is perfect be mine.

Let Thy Knowledge *here* grow in me, and in the world to come be full. Let Thy Love grow *here*, and *there* be fulfilled; that *here* my joy may in hope be great, and *there* indeed find true consummation.

For this let my soul hunger, my flesh thirst after, my whole substance long for, until Thou call me to enter into the Eternal Joy of my LORD, the Trinity

in Unity, GOD, blessed for evermore.
Amen.

HOW plenteous is Thy goodness, O
LORD, which Thou hast secretly
laid up for those that fear Thee !
When I call to mind, O LORD, with
what devotion and affection some holy
souls draw near to Thy Sacrament, then
I am grieved and ashamed that I ap-
proach Thine Altar with so much cold-
ness, that I remain so dry, and indevout
and heartless, that I am not wholly in-
flamed in Thy Presence, O GOD, nor so
tenderly affected as Thy Saints have been.
For they, from excessive desire, and
ardent feeling of love, were unable to
restrain themselves from weeping. With
all their hearts, and with their inmost
being, they panted after Thee, O GOD,
the Fountain of Life, the Nourishment
and Refreshment of holy souls. Yea, so
greatly did they desire Thee, that they
were unable to satisfy their longings save
by receiving and feeding upon Thy Sacred
Body and Blood.
O truly ardent faith of theirs ! existing
as a credible proof of Thy Very Presence.
For they really know their LORD in
the Breaking of Bread whose hearts so
mightily burn within them from the fact
that JESUS walks with them.

Alas ! such affection, such devotion, is very far from me.

Be merciful to me, O good JESUS, kind and gracious One ; grant me such an increase of devotion as shall seem good in Thy sight for the needs of my soul ; that my faith may be strengthened, my hope fortified, and my love more deeply kindled.

I know that Thy Mercy is able to give me the grace I desire, and to visit me with the spirit of devotion when the day of Thy good pleasure shall arrive.

For through Thy grace I desire to attain unto the beatitude of Thy most faithful lovers, and to be numbered with their holy company.

And Thou wilt do for me above what I can ask or think, more than I deserve or know how to desire.

O THOU Blessed LORD JESUS, Who hast now vouchsafed to come under my roof, I most humbly beseech Thee, leave me not, but abide with me for ever. Abide with me, LORD, in all I say, think, do, fear, hope, and enjoy. I fear my own unsteadfastness,—abide with me, LORD, for in Thee there is no change. I often despond, and fear I shall fall ; abide with me, LORD, and make me to feel Thy near-

ness.   Be Thou my Refreshment in weariness ; my Comfort in trouble ; my Refuge
in temptation ; in death my Life ; in judgment my Redeemer.   Abide with me
always, that I may abide in Thee, O good
JESUS, Thou GOD of my Salvation.

*Additional Devotions for use during the
Divine Office will be found in Part III.*

¶ *When all have communicated, the Minister
shall return to the LORD'S Table, and rever-
ently place upon it what remaineth of the
Consecrated Elements, covering the same with
a fair linen cloth.*

¶ *Then shall the Priest say the LORD'S Prayer,
the people repeating after him every Petition.*

OUR FATHER, Which art in heaven, Hallowed be Thy Name.   Thy kingdom come.
Thy will be done in earth, As it is in heaven.
Give us this day our daily bread.   And forgive
us our trespasses, As we forgive them that trespass against us.   And lead us not into temptation ; But deliver us from evil : For Thine is the
kingdom, The power, and the glory, For ever and
ever. Amen.

¶ *After shall be said as followeth.*

O LORD and heavenly FATHER, we Thy
humble servants entirely desire Thy fatherly
goodness mercifully to accept this our sacrifice

of praise and thanksgiving ; most humbly beseeching Thee to grant, that by the merits and
death of Thy SON JESUS CHRIST, and through
faith in His Blood, we, and all Thy whole Church,
may obtain remission of our sins, and all other
benefits of His Passion.   And here we offer and
present unto Thee, O LORD, ourselves, our souls
and bodies, to be a reasonable, holy, and lively
sacrifice unto Thee ; humbly beseeching Thee,
that all we who are partakers of this holy Communion, may be fulfilled with Thy grace and
heavenly benediction.   And although we be unworthy, through our manifold sins, to offer unto
Thee any sacrifice, yet we beseech Thee to accept
this our bounden duty and service ; not weighing
our merits, but pardoning our offences, through
JESUS CHRIST our LORD ; by Whom, and with
Whom, in the unity of the HOLY GHOST, all
honour and glory be unto Thee, O FATHER
Almighty, world without end.   *Amen.*

¶ *Or this.*

A LMIGHTY and everliving GOD, we most
heartily thank Thee, for that Thou dost
vouchsafe to feed us, who have duly received
these holy mysteries, with the spiritual food of
the most precious Body and Blood of Thy SON
our SAVIOUR JESUS CHRIST ; and dost assure us
thereby of Thy favour and goodness towards us ;
and that we are very members incorporate in the
mystical Body of Thy SON, which is the blessed

company of all faithful people ; and are also heirs
through hope of Thy everlasting kingdom, by the
merits of the most Precious Death and Passion of
Thy dear SON.   And we most humbly beseech
Thee, O heavenly FATHER, so to assist us with
Thy grace, that we may continue in that holy
fellowship, and do all such good works as Thou
hast prepared for us to walk in ; through JESUS
CHRIST our LORD, to Whom, with Thee and the
HOLY GHOST, be all honour and glory, world
without end, *Amen.*

¶ Then shall be said or sung,

GLORY be to GOD on high, and in earth
peace, good will towards men.   We praise
Thee, we bless Thee, we worship Thee, we glorify
Thee, we give thanks to Thee for Thy great
glory, O LORD GOD, heavenly King, GOD the
FATHER Almighty.

O LORD, the only-begotten SON JESU CHRIST;
O LORD GOD, LAMB of GOD, SON of the
FATHER, that takest away the sins of the world,
have mercy upon us.   Thou that takest away the
sins of the world, have mercy upon us.   Thou
that takest away the sins of the world, receive our
prayer.   Thou that sittest at the right hand of
GOD the FATHER, have mercy upon us.
• For Thou only art holy, Thou only art the
LORD ; Thou only, O CHRIST, with the HOLY
GHOST, art most high in the glory of GOD the
FATHER. *Amen.*

¶ *Then the Priest (or Bishop, if he be present),
shall let them depart with this Blessing.*

THE peace of GOD, which passeth all understanding, keep your hearts and minds in
the knowledge and love of GOD, and of His SON
JESUS CHRIST our LORD ; and the blessing of
GOD Almighty, the FATHER, the SON, and the
HOLY GHOST, be amongst you and remain with
you always. *Amen.*

After the Blessing.

O ALMIGHTY and Everlasting LORD
GOD, JESUS CHRIST our LORD, be
merciful unto my sins, through the par-
taking of Thy Body and Blood ; for Thou
hast spoken, saying, 'Whoso eateth My
Flesh, and drinketh My Blood, dwelleth
in Me and I in him.' Wherefore I
humbly beseech Thee to create in me a
clean heart, and renew a right spirit
within me ; and deign to stablish me
with Thy free Spirit, and to deliver me
from all the snares and malice of the
devil, that I may be found worthy to
have a share in the joys of heaven ; Who
livest and reignest with the FATHER and
the HOLY GHOST for ever.

I render thanks to Thee, O most sweet
LORD JESU CHRIST, very Light, Health
of believers, Comfort of the sorrowful,
Hope of men, Joy of Angels, that Thou

hast vouchsafed this day to feed me, a sinner, with Thy most sacred Body and Blood. Wherefore I pray that this mysterious and blessed Communion turn not to the condemnation of my soul, but aid me in driving out all the snares and frauds of the devil, so that none of his iniquities may ever have dominion in my heart, body, soul, or senses ; but let Thy gracious favour bring me to the heavenly Banquet of the Angels, where Thou dost dwell, Who art True Blessedness, Light Unclouded, and Everlasting Joy. Amen.

[*If you have not Communicated, you may pray as follows :*

GRANT, we beseech Thee, Almighty GOD, that the words, which we have heard this day with our outward ears, may through Thy grace be so grafted inwardly in our hearts, that they may bring forth in us the fruit of good living, to the honour and praise of Thy Name ; through JESUS CHRIST our LORD. Amen.

Almighty GOD, Who hast promised to hear the petitions of them that ask in Thy SON'S Name ; We beseech Thee mercifully to incline Thine ears to us that have made now our prayers and supplications unto Thee ; and grant, that those things, which we have faithfully asked according to Thy will, may effectually be obtained, to the relief of our necessity, and to the setting forth of Thy Glory ; through JESUS CHRIST our LORD. Amen.

We beseech Thee, O LORD, pour Thy grace into our hearts ; that, as we have known the Incarnation of Thy SON JESUS CHRIST by the message of an Angel, so by His Cross and Passion we may be brought unto the Glory of His Resurrection, through the same JESUS CHRIST our LORD. Amen.]

Ant. The LORD hath given strength unto His people ; the LORD hath given His people the Blessing of Peace.

Nunc dimittis.

LORD, now lettest Thou Thy servant depart in peace : according to Thy word.

For mine eyes have seen : Thy salvation,

Which Thou hast prepared : before the face of all people ;

To be a light to lighten the Gentiles : and to be the glory of Thy people Israel.

Glory be to the FATHER, and to the SON : and to the HOLY GHOST ;

As it was in the beginning, is now, and ever shall be : world without end. Amen.

Ant. The LORD hath given strength unto His people; the LORD hath given His people the Blessing of Peace.

Let us depart in peace ✠ in the Name of the LORD.

On your way home you may say this Gospel.

IN the beginning was the WORD, and the WORD was with GOD, and the WORD was GOD. The same was in the beginning with GOD. All things were made by Him; and without Him was not any thing made that was made. In Him was Life, and the Life was the Light of men. And the Light shineth in darkness, and the darkness comprehended it not. There was a man sent from GOD, whose name was John. The same came for a witness, to bear witness of the Light, that all men through Him might believe. He was not that Light, but was sent to bear witness of that Light. That was the true Light, Which lighteth every man that cometh into the world. He was in the world, and the world was made by Him, and the world knew Him not. He came unto His own, and His own received Him not. But as many as received Him, to them gave He power to become the sons of GOD, even to them that believe on His Name : which were born, not of blood, nor of the will of the flesh, nor of the will of man, but of GOD. And the WORD was made flesh, and dwelt among us (and we beheld His glory, the glory as of the Only-begotten of the FATHER) full of grace and truth.

Additional Devotions for Use during the Celebration of Holy Communion.

Whatsoever ye shall ask in My Name, that will I do, that the FATHER may be glorified in the SON.

Acts of Adoration, etc.

HAIL for evermore, most holy Flesh of CHRIST, to me before all and above all the highest Source of Joy. The Body of our LORD JESUS CHRIST be unto me, a sinner, the Way and the Life; in the Name of the FATHER, and of the SON, and of the HOLY GHOST. Amen.

Hail for evermore, Heavenly Drink, to me before all and above all the highest Source of Joy. The Body and Blood of our LORD JESUS CHRIST be unto me a perpetual healing unto everlasting life; in the Name of the FATHER, and of the SON, and of the HOLY GHOST. Amen.

I will sing the mercies of the LORD for ever.

Who shall separate me from the Love of CHRIST?

O good LORD JESU! suffer me not to be separated from Thee!

Whom have I in heaven but Thee? or what upon earth do I desire apart from

Thee? GOD of my heart, and my Portion for ever.

Deal Thou with me, O LORD GOD, according unto Thy Name, for sweet is Thy Mercy.

Shew Thy marvellous Loving-kindness, Thou that art the SAVIOUR of them which put their trust in Thee.

Salvation belongeth unto the LORD, and Thy Blessing is upon Thy people.

Be Thou exalted, LORD, in Thine own Strength, so will we sing and praise Thy Power.

O GOD the FATHER, Fount and Source of all goodness, Who, moved by Thy Loving-kindness, didst will Thine Only-begotten SON to descend for us to this lower world, and to take our Flesh; I worship Thee, I glorify Thee, I praise Thee with the whole purpose of my mind and heart, and I beseech Thee not to forsake us Thy servants, but to forgive us our sins, that so we may be enabled to serve Thee, the Only True GOD, with a pure heart and chaste body, through the same JESUS CHRIST our LORD.

O LORD JESU CHRIST, SON of the Living GOD, Who by the will of the FATHER, and the co-operation of the HOLY GHOST, hast by Thy Death given life unto the world; deliver me, I beseech

Thee, by this Thy most holy Body and Blood, from all my iniquities and from every evil ; make me ever obedient to Thy commandments, and suffer me never to be separated from Thee ; Who with GOD the FATHER and the same HOLY GHOST livest and reignest GOD, world without end. Amen.

A PRAYER OF S. ANSELM,

Commemorating the Mysteries of the Incarnation.

O LORD JESU, most Benign, Fountain of Life, of Whom all Thy Saints drink, and are filled with unspeakable sweetness, and live in everlasting satiety ; grant Thou to me in this present life ever so to thirst after Thee, that in the Life to come, with the same Thy Saints, I may be counted worthy to be everlastingly satisfied by Thee. Wherefore, I pray Thy most sweet Mercy, O most Loving, most Sweet LORD JESU, feed my wretched soul with the remembrance of Thy Benefits, that it faint not, wearied in its pilgrimage under the weight of its sins.

Thy Goodness, LORD, created me, and by Thy Baptism re-created me, and patiently thus far waiteth for me daily sinning. The power of Thy Godhead made me ; the humiliation of Thy Manhood re-made me.

Behold, O LORD JESU, by the Gift of Thy Grace, Who art my LORD and my GOD, behold I remember that, as Thou didst foretell by Thy holy ones from the beginning of the world, Thou wast Born of a holy Virgin, and of her didst take true Flesh, truly didst suck the breasts of a Virgin Mother. Feed Thou my sinful soul with Thy holy Flesh ; satisfy it with Thy Sweetness.

Thou wast wrapped in swaddling-clothes and laid in a manger : wrap Thou my soul in the swaddling-clothes of Thy Mercy, that it remain not naked before Thee.

The shepherds and the wise men from the East came and worshipped Thee, lying helpless in Thy Mother's arms : make me, LORD, faithfully to worship Thee, now sitting in Heaven.

Thou didst suffer Thy Flesh to be circumcised : circumcise my heart from all sin.

Thou wast presented in the Temple ; Simeon took Thee in his arms : present Thou me to Thy Holy Majesty, that I may embrace Thee with the arms of my soul.

Thou wast subject to Thy parents in Thy childhood : make me subject to

Thee, and to all to whom Thy disposal hast subjected me.

Thou wast baptized by John : in my infancy Thou didst baptize me ; since that holy Baptism I have been manifoldly polluted : by true confession and penitence, cleanse Thou me.

Thou didst command sinners to repent ; to those who worthily repented Thou didst promise forgiveness : make me so to repent of my sins, that I may become meet to obtain from Thee pardon for them.

Thou didst teach truth, mercy, righteousness : teach Thou my heart and enlighten it, that I may be found worthy to be one of those whom Thou by teaching dost inwardly enlighten.

Thou didst work miracles, wonders, healings on the bodies and souls of men, as it pleased Thee : heal Thou the sicknesses of my soul, for I have sinned against Thee.

Thou didst fast for me : make me to abstain from all sin for love of Thee.

Thou wast hungry for me : make me truly to hunger after Thee, Who art the true Bread.

Thou wast wearied for me : strengthen Thou and refresh the weariness of my soul.

O most sweet and merciful LORD JESU CHRIST, when Thou didst sup with Thy friends, Thou didst wash their feet, and

feed them with Thy Body and Thy Blood:
wash Thou my body and soul from all
defilement, and with the same Thy Body
and Thy Blood strengthen them, lest
they faint.

What shall I more say, O LORD JESU
CHRIST? Thou art my Life, my Health,
my Sweetness, my Strength, my Joy, my
Gladness, my Redemption, my Resurrection.

Thou wast delivered up for me : deliver
not up my soul to the enemies.

Thou wast bound for me : loosen Thou
the bonds of my sins.

Thou wast mocked for me : deliver me
from the mockings of the devils.

O most sweet LORD, Thou, Who alone
of men wast without sin, wast scourged
for me : deliver me from the scourges
which mine iniquities have deserved.

O most merciful LORD, Thou wast
crowned with thorns for my sake : take
away from me the thorns of my sins.

O most kind JESU, Thou didst bear
Thy Cross upon Thy holy Shoulders :
make me to follow Thee, and to bear my
soul after Thee.

O most high LORD, lifted up upon the
Cross, Thou didst draw all things unto
Thee : draw Thou me to Thee.

O most gentle LORD, Thou didst suffer
Thy Hands and Thy Feet to be pierced

with iron nails, Thy Side to be opened with the spear, Thy Blood to be shed for sinners : by that Thy Blood wash Thou my soul from all sins, and take away from it all its grief by the anguish which for us Thou didst sustain.

Thou wast given vinegar to drink for me : fill Thou my soul with the honey of Thy sweetness.

Thou didst lay down Thy Life for Thy sheep : suffer not my sinful soul to perish and die.

Thou didst free from hell the souls of the righteous : free Thou my soul from the damnation of the unrighteous.

O most mighty, most powerful LORD JESU CHRIST, after Thou hadst conquered death Thou didst rise from the dead, and didst appear to Thy disciples, alive and immortal. As they grieved for Thy Death, Thou didst gladden them ; eating and drinking often with them, Thou didst stablish their hearts in the faith of Thy holy Resurrection : gladden Thou and strengthen my heart, the heart of Thy servant, in the mystery of Thy victorious Rising from the dead. Amen.

A PRAYER AND INTERCESSION.

O LORD GOD, FATHER ALMIGHTY, Who hast promised rewards to the just, and pardon to the penitent, Who

wouldest not the death of sinners, neither
hast pleasure in the destruction of any that
die ; I humbly entreat Thee to grant unto
us Thy servants remission of all our sins,
and bring us to that penitence by which
Thou didst save David, didst look graciously upon Peter when he wept, and didst
cleanse Mary Magdalene. O LORD JESU
CHRIST, cast out of my heart all things
which offend Thee, and pour into me such
love that I may be enabled perfectly to
love and fear Thee, and neither to think
nor desire anything save that which I
know to be pleasing unto Thee, O LORD.
I commend unto Thee all who love or care
for me, all who give me pitying aid, all
who are indebted to me or related to me.
(And likewise for mine enemies, I beseech
Thee that Thou wouldest turn them unto
peace, and bring them to true penitence.)
I entreat Thee also mercifully to remember all who are mindful of me, and who
have commended themselves to my unworthy prayers, and who have done me
any charity or kindness : as well as all
those who are connected with me by
friendship or the bonds of faith, whether
they be still in the body or have departed
this life . . . and visit them, that they,
faithfully serving Thee, may be defended
from all adversities ; and grant unto them
and me deliverance from all punishment,

and bring us to everlasting rest. And
this I earnestly implore, that whenever the
day of my death shall come, Thou Thyself, Who givest judgment against the
accusers, wilt become my Defender : Who
art Blessed for ever and ever. Amen.

PSALM V. Verba mea auribus.

PONDER my words, O LORD : consider my meditation.

O hearken Thou unto the voice of my
calling, my King, and my GOD : for unto
Thee will I make my prayer.

My voice shalt Thou hear betimes, O
LORD : early in the morning will I direct
my prayer unto Thee, and will look up.

For Thou art the GOD that hast no
pleasure in wickedness : neither shall any
evil dwell with Thee.

Such as be foolish shall not stand in
Thy sight : for Thou hatest all them that
work vanity.

Thou shalt destroy them that speak
leasing : the LORD will abhor both the
blood-thirsty and deceitful man.

But as for me, I will come into Thine
house, even upon the multitude of Thy
mercy : and in Thy fear will I worship
toward Thy holy temple.

Lead me, O LORD, in Thy righteousness,
because of mine enemies : make Thy way
plain before my face.

For there is no faithfulness in his mouth : their inward parts are very wickedness.

Their throat is an open sepulchre : they flatter with their tongue.

Destroy Thou them, O GOD ; let them perish through their own imaginations : cast them out in the multitude of their ungodliness ; for they have rebelled against Thee.

And let all them that put their trust in Thee rejoice : they shall ever be giving of thanks, because Thou defendest them ; they that love Thy Name shall be joyful in Thee ;

For Thou, LORD, wilt give Thy blessing unto the righteous : and with Thy favourable kindness wilt Thou defend him as with a shield.

Glory be to the FATHER, and to the SON : and to the HOLY GHOST ;

As it was in the beginning, is now, and ever shall be : world without end.   Amen.

PSALM CXVI.   Dilexi, quoniam.

I AM well pleased : that the LORD hath heard the voice of my prayer ;

That He hath inclined His ear unto me : therefore will I call upon Him as long as I live.

The snares of death compassed me round about : and the pains of hell gat hold upon me.

I shall find trouble and heaviness, and I will call upon the Name of the LORD: O LORD, I beseech Thee, deliver my soul.

Gracious is the LORD, and righteous: yea, our GOD is merciful.

The LORD preserveth the simple: I was in misery, and He helped me.

Turn again then unto thy rest, O my soul: for the LORD hath rewarded thee.

And why? Thou hast delivered my soul from death: mine eyes from tears, and my feet from falling.

I will walk before the LORD: in the land of the living.

I believed, and therefore will I speak; but I was sore troubled: I said in my haste, All men are liars.

What reward shall I give unto the LORD: for all the benefits that He hath done unto me?

I will receive the cup of salvation: and call upon the Name of the LORD.

I will pay my vows now in the presence of all His people: right dear in the sight of the LORD is the death of His saints.

Behold, O LORD, how that I am Thy servant: I am Thy servant, and the son of Thine handmaid; Thou hast broken my bonds in sunder.

I will offer to Thee the sacrifice of thanksgiving: and will call upon the Name of the LORD.

I will pay my vows unto the LORD, in the sight of all His people : in the courts of the LORD'S house, even in the midst of thee, O Jerusalem.   Praise the LORD.

Glory be to the FATHER, and to the SON : and to the HOLY GHOST ;

As it was in the beginning, is now, and ever shall be : world without end.   Amen.

Benedicite, omnia Opera.

O ALL ye Works of the LORD, bless ye the LORD : praise Him, and magnify Him for ever.

O ye Angels of the LORD, bless ye the LORD : praise Him, and magnify Him for ever.

O ye Heavens, bless ye the LORD : praise Him, and magnify Him for ever.

O let the Earth bless the LORD : yea, let it praise Him, and magnify Him for ever.

O ye Children of Men, bless ye the LORD : praise Him, and magnify Him for ever.

O let Israel bless the LORD : praise Him, and magnify Him for ever.

O ye Priests of the LORD, bless ye the LORD : praise Him, and magnify Him for ever.

O ye Servants of the LORD, bless ye the LORD : praise Him, and magnify Him for ever.

O ye Spirits and Souls of the Righteous, bless ye the LORD : praise Him, and magnify Him for ever.

O ye holy and humble Men of heart, bless ye the LORD : praise Him, and magnify Him for ever.

O Ananias, Azarias, and Misael, bless ye the LORD : praise Him, and magnify Him for ever.

Glory be to the FATHER, and to the SON : and to the HOLY GHOST ;

As it was in the beginning, is now, and ever shall be : world without end. Amen.

HYMNS.

I.

RHYTHM OF S. THOMAS AQUINAS.

I ADORE Thee truly, hidden DEITY,
    Outward signs Thou givest, GOD we cannot see,
All my heart surrenders unto Thee alone
In that contemplation, self for ever gone.
Sight, and touch, and tasting, fail the truth to
    find,
But the faith, by hearing, penetrates the mind.
I believe whatever GOD's own SON hath taught,
Nothing can be truer than the Word He
    brought.
On the Cross the Godhead veiled Its awful
    light ;
Here, no less the Manhood hides from mortal
    sight :

Both alike confessing, with entire belief,
Now I pray, as near Thee prayed the dying
     thief.
To Thy Wounds, like Thomas, here I may
     not press ;
Yet, my GOD, I know Thee, and my LORD
     confess.
Make me to believe Thee ever more and more,
Hope in Thee supremely, love Thee, and
     adore !
O Memorial Offering of Thy Death, my LORD !
Living Bread Celestial, Life to man restored,
Grant my mind its longing, thus on Thee to
     live,
And to me that sweetness ever deign to give.
Since, O Sacred JESU ! I from Thee am fed,
Cleanse me from pollution, by Thy Blood once
     shed ;
One pure drop descending might suffice to win
All the world's salvation from the curse of
     sin.
JESU, Who art hidden from these eyes of
     mine,
Give to me, I pray Thee, that for which I
     pine,
All unveiled to know Thee, face to face adore,
Blessed in that vision, glory evermore !

II.

HIGH on His Altar Throne, behold
     Our great EMMANUEL,
In Sacramental robe arrayed,
     Now deigns with man to dwell !

He Who once made our peace with God
　On Calvary's cross-crowned hill,
Presents that selfsame Sacrifice
　For man's Redemption still.

In Heaven above, on earth below,
　He stands our One HIGH PRIEST,
His Great Atonement pleads for us
　In every Eucharist !

His Blood He gives, to cleanse from sin,
　His Flesh, to be our stay,
And with Himself with His own Hand
　He feeds us day by day.

So evermore He dwells in us
　That we in Him may live,
And yield ourselves to GOD, as He
　Himself for man doth give.

By this Pure Offering sanctified,
　O Victim-Priest Divine,
Receive our worthless sacrifice,
　And offer it with Thine.

Sealed with His Cross, robed in His grace
　Bought with His Blood unpriced,
Behold us, FATHER, in Thy SON,
　Accept us in our CHRIST !

III.

WHEN I survey the wondrous Cross
　On which the Prince of Glory died.
My richest gain I count but loss,
　And pour contempt on all my pride.

Forbid it, LORD, that I should boast
   Save in the Cross of CHRIST, my GOD ;
All the vain things that charm me most
   I sacrifice them to His Blood.

See from His Head, His Hands, His Feet,
   Sorrow and love flow mingling down ;
Did e'er such love and sorrow meet,
   Or thorns compose so rich a crown ?

Were the whole realm of nature mine,
   That were an offering far too small ;
Love so amazing, so Divine,
   Demands my soul, my life, my all !

To CHRIST, Who won for sinners grace,
   By bitter grief and anguish sore,
Be praise from all the ransomed race,
   For ever and for evermore.

IV.

DRAWN to the Cross which Thou hast
     blessed
With healing gifts for souls distressed,
To find in Thee my Life, my Rest,
      CHRIST Crucified, I come.

Stained with the sins which I have wrought,
In word and deed and secret thought,
For Pardon which Thy Blood hath bought,
      CHRIST Crucified, I come.

Weary of selfishness and pride,
False pleasures gone, vain hopes denied,
Deep in Thy Wounds my shame to hide,
      CHRIST Crucified, I come.

Thou knowest all my griefs and fears,
Thy grace abused, my misspent years,
Yet now to Thee, for cleansing tears,
    CHRIST Crucified, I come.

I would not, if I could, conceal
The ills which only Thou canst heal,
So to the Cross, where sinners kneel,
    CHRIST Crucified, I come.

Wash me, and take away each stain,
Let nothing of my sin remain,
For cleansing, though it be through pain,
    CHRIST Crucified, I come.

And then for work to do for Thee,
Which shall so sweet a penance be
That angels well might envy me,
    CHRIST Crucified, I come.

A life of labour, prayers, and love,
Which shall my heart's conversion prove,
Till to a glorious Rest above,
    CHRIST Crucified, I come.

To share with Thee Thy Life Divine,
Thy Righteousness, Thy Likeness mine,
Since Thou hast made my nature Thine,
    CHRIST Crucified, I come.

To be what Thou wouldst have me be,
Accepted, sanctified in Thee,
Through what Thy grace shall work in me,
    CHRIST Crucified, I come.

V.

I GAVE My Life for thee,
   My Precious Blood I shed
That thou might'st ransomed be
   And quickened from the dead.
I gave My Life for thee :
What hast thou given for Me ?

I spent long years for thee
   In weariness and woe,
That an eternity
   Of joy thou mightest know.
I spent long years for thee :
Hast thou spent one for Me ?

My FATHER'S Home of light,
   My rainbow-circled Throne
I left, for earthly night,
   For wanderings sad and lone.
I left it all for thee :
Hast thou left aught for Me ?

I suffered much for thee,
   More than thy tongue may tell
Of bitterest agony,
   To rescue thee from hell.
I suffered much for thee :
What canst thou bear for Me ?

And I have brought to thee,
   Down from My Home above,
Salvation full and free,
   My Pardon, and My Love.
Great gifts I brought to thee :
What hast thou brought to Me ?

Oh ! let thy life be given,
   Thy years for Him be spent,
World-fetters all be riven,
   And joy with suffering blent.
Bring thou thy worthless all ;
Follow thy SAVIOUR's call.

VI.

HARK, my soul ! it is the LORD ;
   'Tis thy SAVIOUR, hear His word ;
JESUS speaks, and speaks to thee,
' Say, poor sinner, lov'st thou Me ?

' I delivered thee when bound,
And, when bleeding, healed thy wound ;
Sought thee wandering, set thee right,
Turned thy darkness into light.

' Can a woman's tender care
Cease towards the child she bare ?
Yes, she may forgetful be,
Yet will I remember thee.

' Mine is an unchanging Love,
Higher than the heights above ;
Deeper than the depths beneath,
Free and faithful, strong as death.

' Thou shalt see My Glory soon,
When the work of grace is done,
Partner of My Throne shalt be ;—
Say, poor sinner, lov'st thou Me ?'

LORD, it is my chief complaint
That my love is weak and faint,
Yet I love Thee, and adore,—
Oh for grace to love Thee more !

VII.

FOR ever here my rest shall be,
    Close to Thy Bleeding Side ;
This all my hope and all my plea,
    For me the SAVIOUR died.

My dying SAVIOUR and my GOD,
    Fountain for guilt and sin,
Sprinkle me ever with Thy Blood,
    And cleanse, and keep me clean.

Wash me, and make me thus Thine own,
    Wash me, and mine Thou art ;
Wash me, but not my feet alone,
    My hands, my head, my heart.

The Atonement of Thy Blood apply,
    Till Faith to sight improve ;
Till Hope in full fruition die,
    And all my soul be Love.

*The following Hymns, A. and M., will also
be found helpful to devotion during this time:*
—164, 178, 182, 191, 304, 313, 316, 322, 323.

INTERCESSION.

*This time is specially suitable for ear-
nest pleading with GOD on behalf of souls
for whom CHRIST died. The following*

heads of Intercession are here given as helps in the right performance of this duty.

I.

Pray—For parents [*husband, wife, children, brothers, sisters*], other relatives.

Those who have done us good by their prayers, or in any other way.

Those whom we have injured by example or neglect.

Friends, especially . . . [*Here recall their names and think of their several necessities.*]

Those who are unkind to us, or whom we find it difficult to get on with.

II.

Pray—For godchildren . . . [*Here name them.*]

Candidates preparing for Holy Baptism.

Unbaptised infants.

Those who neglect Baptism.

The newly baptised.

Candidates for Confirmation.

The newly confirmed.

III.

Pray—For devout Communicants.

Formal and infrequent Communicants.

Those who abstain from Communion through a sense of unworthiness.

Persons preparing for a First Communion.

For the increase of daily Celebrations.

For penitents desiring to make their peace with GOD.

Those who shrink from the pain of a true repentance.

IV.

Pray—For all those engaged in teaching, or who are being trained to teach.

All scholars ; especially those in public schools or colleges.

Men of science.

Persons in position of trust or danger.

Labourers and artisans.

Children and young people employed in factories.

V.

Pray—For all infidels . . . schismatics . . .

Persons troubled with doubts, or unwilling to know the Truth.
Christian members of irreligious households.
The worldly and careless.
The rich and prosperous.

VI.

Pray—For all in sickness, who have none to be kind to them . . . For those in their last agony . . .
Other sick people . . . confirmed invalids . . .
Those who minister to them.
Persons in bereavement . . . poverty . . . loneliness . . . sorrow of heart . . . distress of mind . . .

VII.

Pray—For all persons living in sin.
Those in temptation.
The children of wicked people.
The uncared-for children of great cities.
Children in workhouses.
Prisoners, and persons condemned to death.
Drunkards.
Impenitent and hardened sinners.

VIII.

Pray—For those in authority in the State.
>   The Bishops of the Universal
>   Church, especially . . .
>   All Priests and Deacons . . .
>   Missionary and Colonial Churches
>   . . . Religious Houses, Guilds,
>   and Orders.
>   All persons engaged in the ser-
>   vices of the Church.

IX.

Pray—For religious heathen.
>   The inhabitants of unexplored
>   regions, and of the isles which
>   to this day are waiting for the
>   revelation of GOD in CHRIST.
>   For the heathen in our midst.
>   Home Missions . . . especially . . .

X.

Pray—For those upon whose work and
>   service we depend.
>   Servants of our household.
>   Those whom we employ in any
>   other way.
>   Railway and government officials.

Prayers for Special Occasions.

For a Birthday Anniversary.

O GOD, Who didst deign to create me for Thy service, and didst breathe into me the breath of life, that living I might praise Thee; I glorify Thee for the life which Thou hast given, and I pray Thee that by the Blessed Sacrament of Thy dear SON, Thou wilt preserve and sanctify me to a blessed immortality, that when CHRIST, Who is my Life, shall appear, I may also appear with Him in Glory; Who liveth and reigneth with Thee and the HOLY GHOST, for ever and ever. Amen.

For the Anniversary of Baptism.

O HEAVENLY FATHER, Who, as on this day didst vouchsafe to regenerate me, and to incorporate me into the Body of Thy SON CHRIST our LORD; grant, that as I have been buried with Him in Baptism, so by this Holy Communion I may rise with Him to glorious and perfect Life, that at the last He may present me faultless in Thy Presence with exceeding joy, through the Grace which His Death and Resurrection have won for me ; Who liveth and reigneth with Thee, in the Unity of the HOLY GHOST, Blessed for evermore.   Amen.

For the Anniversary of First Communion.

O LORD JESU CHRIST, Who camest down from Heaven to give life unto the world, and Who, as on this sacred day, didst first receive me to the Holy Communion of Thy Love ; I thank Thee for all the blessings which Thou hast bestowed upon me in Thy Life-giving Eucharist, and I pray Thee that by Thy Grace indwelling me, I may lead on earth a life of purity and peace, and may hereafter attain to the blessedness of Everlasting Communion with Thee ; Who with the FATHER and the HOLY GHOST livest and reignest for ever and ever.   Amen.

At a Marriage.

O GOD, Whose Blessed SON hath imparted to the bond of Marriage a Sacramental significance by His Mysti-

cal Union with the Church His Bride;
vouchsafe unto Thy servants [*N.N.*] now
solemnising their Marriage in this Holy
Communion, so to live together in this
world, that they may be accounted
worthy to attain to the world to come;
through the same Thy SON JESUS CHRIST
our LORD. Amen.

At a Communion of the Sick.

O CHRIST, Physician of souls, and
Medicine of immortality, come near
to this Thy servant, and visit *him* with
Thy Salvation. Let Thy Holy Sacrament be to *him* for the strengthening and
refreshing of *his* body, and for the healing of *his* soul, that being raised from *his*
bed of sickness, *he* may walk before Thee
in renewed strength and holiness of life,
to the glory of Thy Name. Amen.

At a Last Communion.

A LMIGHTY and Everlasting GOD,
Preserver of souls, Who dost cor-
rect those whom Thou dost love, and for
their amendment dost tenderly chastise
those whom Thou dost receive, we call
upon Thee, O LORD, to bestow Thy healing, that the soul of Thy servant at the
hour of *his* departure from the body may
by the hands of Thy holy Angels be pre-

sented without spot unto Thee. Through
JESUS CHRIST our LORD. Amen.

ASSIST us mercifully, O LORD, in our
supplications, and receive the Oblation which we offer to Thee in behalf of
Thy servant who seeketh the health not
of *his* body, but of *his* soul : grant *him*,
we beseech Thee, pardon of all *his* sins ;
that through this Sacrifice which we present to Thee, *his* soul may be received by
the holy Angels, and be counted worthy
to attain to the Kingdom of Thy Glory.
Through JESUS CHRIST our LORD.
Amen.

At a Funeral.

LOOK down, we beseech Thee, Almighty GOD, and vouchsafe favourably to receive this Sacrifice which we
offer unto Thee in behalf of the soul of
Thy servant [*N.*] ; and grant *him* perpetual peace and everlasting rest. Through
JESUS CHRIST our LORD. Amen.

WE beseech Thee, O LORD, let the
Celebration of the Divine Sacrament be profitable unto the soul of Thy
servant [*N.*], that of Thy Mercy *he* may
have eternal fellowship with Him in
Whom *he* trusted and believed. Through
JESUS CHRIST our LORD. Amen.

For those at Sea.

O GOD, Who didst bring Thy chosen people through the Red Sea, and bear them through the great waters ; we praise Thy Name, and humbly beseech Thee to vouchsafe to turn away all adversities from Thy servants at sea, and to bring them with a calm voyage to the haven where they would be. Through JESUS CHRIST our LORD. Amen.

In Time of War.

O GOD, the Sovereign of all Kings and Kingdoms, Who by smiting healest, and by forgiving sparest us ; extend unto us Thy Mercy, that we may use for our restoration and correction the peace and quietness established by Thy Power. Through JESUS CHRIST our LORD. Amen.

For one in Trouble of Heart.

O GOD, Who healest those that are broken in heart, and turnest the sadness of the sorrowful to joy ; favourably look upon this Offering by which Thou willest to remit the sins of the whole world, and mercifully accept it for Thy servant [*N.*] in *his* trouble ; pardon all *his* sins, banish *his* cares, and remove *his* straits and affliction, that *he*, being delivered from all the evils which *he* suffers, may evermore delight in giving thanks for Thy blessings.   Through JESUS CHRIST our LORD.   Amen.

In time of Common Sickness.

ALMIGHTY and Merciful GOD, look upon the people now lying under the hand of Thy Majesty ; and let the receiving of Thy Holy Sacrament prevent the deadly sickness from overtaking us. Through JESUS CHRIST our LORD. Amen.

For one going on a Journey.

O GOD of infinite Mercy and boundless Majesty, Whom neither space nor time divides from those whom Thou defendest ; be present with Thy servant who in all places putteth *his* trust in Thee, and vouchsafe to be *his* Guide and Companion in every way by which *he* is going ; let no adversity harm *him*, no difficulty hinder *him;* let all things be healthful and prosperous for *him*, that whatsoever *he* shall rightly ask, *he* may by the aid of Thy Right Hand speedily and effectually obtain.   Through JESUS CHRIST our LORD.   Amen.

At a Harvest Thanksgiving.

O GOD, Who makest the earth to bring forth her fruits in due season ; receive, we beseech Thee, our Service of Praise and Thanksgiving for the Harvest which Thou hast been pleased to send us, and grant that we, being refreshed with the Bread of Life and the Wine of Salvation, may so live before Thee here, that we may rejoice before Thee in that Day when the reapers shall be the Angels. Through JESUS CHRIST our LORD. Amen.

At a Dedication Festival.

O GOD, Who hast deigned to sanctify this Temple with Thy Glorious Presence ; grant unto us Thy servants so to reverence Thee in this earthly sanctuary, that we may hereafter be found worthy to serve before Thee in the Holiest Place of all. Through JESUS CHRIST our LORD. Amen.

At an Ordination.

POUR down Thy HOLY SPIRIT, O LORD, upon these Thy servants whom Thou callest to minister in the Priesthood of Thy SON ; that by purity of doctrine and holiness of life they may advance the glory of Thy Kingdom, and win souls to Salvation for whom CHRIST died ; Who liveth and reigneth with Thee, in the Unity of the same HOLY SPIRIT, One GOD Blessed for evermore. Amen.

A Thanksgiving.

O GOD, Who shewest Thy Glory by Thy Goodness, and Who lovest all the works of Thy Hands ; we give Thee thanks for all Thy mercies vouch-safed unto us (especially . . .). Receive, we pray Thee, this Holy Sacrifice which we offer unto Thee for a perpetual Eucharist ; and grant that we may ever shew forth in our lives that thankfulness which in our worship we here render unto Thee.   Through JESUS CHRIST our LORD.   Amen.

Collects.

For Use in Advent.

STIR up, we beseech Thee, O LORD, Thy power, and come, that we may be accounted worthy to be rescued by Thy protection, and from the threatening dangers of our sins to be freed by Thy deliverance. Through JESUS CHRIST our LORD. Amen.

GRANT, we beseech Thee, Almighty GOD, that the approaching solemnity of our Redemption may both afford us succour in this present life, and abundantly bestow on us the rewards of Eternal happiness. Through JESUS CHRIST our LORD. Amen.

MAKE haste, we beseech Thee, O LORD, and tarry not; and grant us the assistance of Thy strength from above, that they who trust in Thy goodness may be sustained by the consolations of Thy Coming. Who livest and reignest

with the FATHER and the HOLY GHOST,
One GOD, world without end.   Amen.

GRANT to us, O LORD, Thine unworthy servants, that we who are
cast down by the guilt of our own deeds,
may be gladdened by the Coming of Thy
Only-begotten SON.   Who liveth and
reigneth with Thee and the HOLY GHOST,
One GOD, world without end.   Amen.

Christmas Eve.

GOD, Who makest us glad with the
yearly expectation of our Redemption, grant that as we joyfully receive Thy
Only-begotten SON for our Redeemer,
so we may with sure confidence behold
the same LORD JESUS CHRIST Thy SON,
when He shall come to be our Judge.
Who liveth and reigneth with Thee and
the HOLY GHOST, One GOD, world without end.   Amen.

Christmas.

O GOD, Who hast caused this most
Holy Night to shine with the illu-
mination of the True Light ; grant, we
beseech Thee, that we who have known
the mysteries of this Light on earth, may
likewise obtain the full enjoyment of it in

Heaven. Who liveth and reigneth with Thee and the HOLY GHOST, One GOD, world without end. Amen.

GRANT, we beseech Thee, Almighty GOD, unto us on whom is largely shed the Light of Thy Incarnate Word, that as by faith It enlightened our minds, so It may shine forth in our deeds. Through JESUS CHRIST our LORD. Amen.

GRANT, we beseech Thee, Almighty GOD, that we, who are held in bondage by the old yoke of sin, by the new Birth in the Flesh of Thy Only-begotten may be set free. Through JESUS CHRIST our LORD. Amen.

O ALMIGHTY and Everlasting LORD, direct our actions according to Thy Good Pleasure, that in the Name of Thy Beloved SON we may be deemed worthy to abound in good works. Who liveth and reigneth with Thee and the HOLY GHOST, One GOD, world without end. Amen.

Circumcision.

O GOD, Who permittest us to celebrate the Octave of our SAVIOUR's Birth; vouchsafe, we beseech Thee, that as we are renewed by the Communion of His Flesh, so we may be defended by His Everlasting Divinity. Who liveth and reigneth with Thee and the HOLY GHOST, One GOD, world without end. Amen.

Epiphany.

WE beseech Thee, O LORD, that the brightness of this Festival may enlighten our hearts, that so we may escape from this world, and may come to the land of Eternal Light. Through JESUS CHRIST our LORD. Amen.

WE bring offerings to Thee, O LORD, in honour of the Manifestation of Thy SON ; humbly beseeching Thee, that as the same our LORD JESUS CHRIST is the Author of our gifts, so He may also Himself in mercy graciously accept the same. Who liveth and reigneth with Thee in the Unity of the HOLY GHOST, for ever and ever. Amen.

MAY Thy heavenly Light, we beseech Thee, O LORD, prevent us at all times and in all places ; that we may contemplate with a clear vision, and receive with due effect, the Mystery whereof Thou art pleased we should partake. Through JESUS CHRIST our LORD. Amen.

Lent.

GRACIOUSLY favour us, O LORD, we beseech Thee, in the fast on which we have entered; that the duties which we observe outwardly, we may also be enabled to fulfil with pure minds. Through JESUS CHRIST our LORD. Amen.

GIVE ear, O LORD, to our supplications, and grant that we may with true devotion observe this solemn fast, which was instituted to give health and salvation both to our souls and bodies. Through JESUS CHRIST our LORD. Amen.

CONVERT us, O GOD our SAVIOUR, that this fast of Lent may be beneficial to us, and instruct our minds with Thy heavenly doctrine. Through JESUS CHRIST our LORD. Amen.

ALMIGHTY, Everlasting GOD, Who hast appointed the observance of fasting and almsgiving for the remedy of our sins, mercifully grant us ever to be devoted to Thee in mind and body. Through JESUS CHRIST our LORD. Amen.

Passion-tide.

ALMIGHTY GOD, graciously behold the offerings of Thy faithful people; and grant that the chains of the world may not hold them captive whom by the Passion of Thy SON Thou dost will to be set free. Who liveth and reigneth with Thee and the HOLY GHOST, One GOD, world without end. Amen.

GRANT, we beseech Thee, O Almighty GOD, that we who, by reason of our weakness, faint under so many adversities, may recover by the pleading Passion of Thy Only-begotten SON. Who liveth and reigneth with Thee and the HOLY GHOST, One GOD, world without end. Amen.

Easter.

O GOD, Who didst will Thy SON to suffer Death upon the Cross for us, that Thou mightest cast out of us the power of the enemy; grant to us Thy servants that we may ever live rejoicing in His Resurrection. Through the same Thy SON JESUS CHRIST. Amen.

O GOD, Who dost continually multiply Thy Church with new offspring; grant unto Thy servants that they may hold fast in their lives the Sacrament which they have received by faith. Through JESUS CHRIST our LORD. Amen.

O GOD, Who by the yearly solemnity of the Resurrection of our LORD fillest us with joy; mercifully grant that through the Feasts which we celebrate in this world we may come at last to those joys that are Eternal. Through the same our LORD JESUS CHRIST. Amen.

GRANT, we beseech Thee, Almighty GOD that we who have fulfilled the Paschal Feast, may by Thy bounty hold it fast in our lives and conversation. Through JESUS CHRIST our LORD. Amen.

Rogation Days.

GRANT, we beseech Thee, Almighty GOD, that we who in our afflictions put our trust in Thy goodness, may by Thy protection ever be defended against all adversities. Through JESUS CHRIST, our LORD. Amen.

WE beseech Thee, O LORD, further our prayers with Thy gracious favour; that we, receiving Thy gifts in trouble, may, by reason of the comfort we

find, increase in love to Thee.   Through
JESUS CHRIST our LORD.   Amen.

The Ascension.

GRANT, we beseech Thee, Almighty
FATHER, that our minds may be
ever intent upon that blessed place whither
Thine Only-begotten SON our LORD, the
glorious Author of this Festival, hath gone
before ; that they may in conversation
attain to that towards which by faith they
reach forth.   Through the same JESUS
CHRIST our LORD.   Amen.

GRANT, we beseech Thee, Almighty
GOD, that by this most Holy Communion we may confidently believe that
will be accomplished in the Body of the
whole Church which hath already been
accomplished in her Head.   Through the
same JESUS CHRIST.   Amen.

Whitsuntide.

GRANT, we beseech Thee, Almighty
GOD, that the rays of Thy Brightness may shine upon us ; and that the
Light of Thy Light may, by the illumina-
tion of the HOLY GHOST, strengthen the
hearts of those who have been born again
by Thy Grace.   Through JESUS CHRIST
our LORD.   Amen.

WE beseech Thee, O LORD, let the power of Thy HOLY GHOST come upon us, that it may both cleanse our hearts and defend us from all adversity. Through JESUS CHRIST our LORD. Amen.

Trinity Sunday.

SANCTIFY, we beseech Thee, O LORD GOD, HOLY TRINITY, by the invocation of Thy holy Name, the offering of this Oblation, and through It perfect us to be an eternal gift presented unto Thee. Through JESUS CHRIST our LORD. Amen.

MAY the receiving of this Sacrament, O LORD our GOD, and the confession of the Everlasting HOLY TRINITY, and of the Undivided Unity of the Same, be profitable to us for the salvation of body and soul. Who livest and reignest for ever and ever. Amen.

Thanksgiving

after

Holy Communion.

The Word is very nigh unto thee, in thy mouth and in thy heart.

A Prayer for Grace.

He that hath, to him shall be given.

IN the Name of the ✠ FATHER, and of the SON, and of the HOLY GHOST. Amen.

I thank Thee, O LORD, for the Love Thou hast shewn me once again in admitting me to be a partaker of these Holy Mysteries ; and I pray Thee to forgive whatsoever Thou hast seen amiss in my service to-day, that this Holy Communion be not for my condemnation at the Last Great Day.

And now, O LORD, I beseech Thee, leave me not, but abide with me for ever. Abide with me in weakness, for Thou art my Strength ; in penitence, for Thou art my Peace ; in the bearing of the Cross, for Thou didst hang thereon. Be Thou to me more than my soul desireth, do Thou for me more than I can ask. But chiefly, O LORD, give me a heart pure, obedient, and contented, a devotion untiring in its zeal, a will entirely resigned unto Thine Own.

O Thou Who art able to keep me from
falling, and to present me faultless in the
Presence of Thy Glory with exceeding joy,
have mercy ; and in all the trials of my
life on earth, in the hour of death and
in the Day of Judgment, Good LORD, deliver me.   Amen.

I will go forth in the strength of the
LORD GOD, and will make mention of
Thy Righteousness only.   I will sing of
the LORD, because He hath dealt so lov-
ingly with me ; yea, I will praise the Name
of the LORD most Highest.   Alleluia !

Ephes. vi. 10.

BE strong in the LORD, and in the
power of His might.   Put on the
whole armour of GOD, that ye may be able
to stand against the wiles of the devil.
For we wrestle not against flesh and blood,
but against principalities, against powers,
against the rulers of the darkness of this
world, against spiritual wickedness in high
places.   Wherefore take unto you the
whole armour of GOD, that ye may be
able to withstand in the evil day, and,
having done all, to stand.   Stand, therefore, having your loins girt about with
truth ; and having on the breastplate of
righteousness ; and your feet shod with

the preparation of the gospel of peace ;
above all, taking the shield of faith, wherewith ye shall be able to quench all the
fiery darts of the wicked ; and take the
helmet of salvation, and the sword of the
SPIRIT, which is the Word of GOD : pray-
ing always with all prayer and supplication
in the SPIRIT, and watching thereunto
with all perseverance and supplication for
all saints.

PSALM CXI. Confitebor tibi.

I WILL give thanks unto the LORD
with my whole heart : secretly among
the faithful, and in the congregation.

The works of the LORD are great :
sought out of all them that have pleasure
therein.

His work is worthy to be praised, and
had in honour : and His righteousness
endureth for ever.

The merciful and gracious LORD hath
so done His marvellous works : that they
ought to be had in remembrance.

He hath given meat unto them that
fear Him : He shall ever be mindful of
His covenant.

He hath shewed His people the power
of His works : that He may give them
the heritage of the heathen.

The works of His hands are verity and

judgment : all His commandments are true.

They stand fast for ever and ever : and are done in truth and equity.

He sent redemption unto His people : He hath commanded His covenant for ever ; holy and reverend is His Name.

The fear of the LORD is the beginning of wisdom : a good understanding have all they that do thereafter ; the praise of it endureth for ever.

Glory be to the FATHER, and to the SON : and to the HOLY GHOST ;

As it was in the beginning, is now, and ever shall be : world without end. Amen.

The Abiding Presence.

They constrained Him, saying, Abide with us.

ABIDE with us, LORD; abide with us, even until the morning; let us enjoy meanwhile Thy Presence; let us be glad and rejoice in Thy Resurrection. The darkness thickeneth, evening presseth upon the day. May our Sun, CHRIST our GOD, shew the Light of His Countenance upon us!

O good LORD, I have this day received Thee into my soul; leave me not, O my SAVIOUR, lest, losing Thee, I die. My soul hangeth upon Thee; O LORD, forsake not Thou Thine Own!

Thou hast fed me to-day with that Bread which came down from Heaven, of which he that eateth shall never die; Thou hast given me to drink of that Precious Blood, shed for the Remission of Sins, which maketh our Peace with GOD. Therefore my heart is glad and my glory rejoiceth; my flesh also shall rest in hope.

Thou didst bring me to the Banqueting-

House of Thy Eucharistic Mysteries, and above me Thou didst spread the Banner of Thy Love. There, in the Holiest Place, Thou spakedst to my soul the things that belong to its peace. There, Thou didst refresh me with Thyself, and didst shew me things to come.

Oh stablish the thing which Thou hast wrought in me ! Let me from henceforth walk worthy of the vocation with which I am called, that I grieve not the HOLY SPIRIT of GOD, nor cause Thee to depart from me, by Whose Sacramental Indwelling I am sanctified, and by Whose Life I live.

Forgive me, my SAVIOUR, Longsuffering and Pitiful One, forgive the unworthiness which Thou hast seen in my Communion this day, and for Thy tender mercies' sake impute it not to me for sin.

And now, LORD, abide in me, that I may abide in Thee, as Thou art in the FATHER and the FATHER is in Thee, that I may be one with Thee and with the FATHER, according to Thy Will.

For I am persuaded, that neither death, nor life, nor angels, nor principalities, nor powers, nor things present, nor things to come, nor height, nor depth, nor any other creature, shall be able to separate me from the Love of GOD, which is in CHRIST JESUS our LORD. Amen.

S. John xv. i.

I AM the true Vine, and My FATHER is the Husbandman. Every branch in me that beareth not fruit He taketh away; and every branch that beareth fruit, He purgeth it, that it may bring forth more fruit. Now ye are clean through the word which I have spoken unto you. Abide in Me, and I in you. As the branch cannot bear fruit of itself, except it abide in the vine; no more can ye, except ye abide in Me. I am the Vine, ye are the branches. He that abideth in Me, and I in him, the same bringeth forth much fruit; for without Me ye can do nothing. If a man abide not in Me, he is cast forth as a branch, and is withered; and men gather them, and cast them into the fire, and they are burned. If ye abide in Me, and My words abide in you, ye shall ask what ye will, and it shall be done unto you. Herein is My FATHER glorified, that ye bear much fruit; so shall ye be My disciples. As the FATHER hath loved Me, so have I loved you: continue ye in My love. If ye keep My commandments, ye shall abide in My love; even as I have kept My FATHER'S commandments, and abide in His love. These things have I spoken unto you, that My joy might re-

main in you, and that your joy might be
full.

PSALM LXII. *Nonne Deo?*

MY soul truly waiteth still upon GOD:
for of Him cometh my salvation.

He verily is my Strength and my Salvation : He is my Defence, so that I shall
not greatly fall.

How long will ye imagine mischief
against every man : ye shall be slain all
the sort of you ; yea, as a tottering wall
shall ye be, and like a broken hedge.

Their device is only how to put him
out whom GOD will exalt : their delight
is in lies ; they give good words with
their mouth, but curse with their heart.

Nevertheless, my soul, wait thou still
upon GOD : for my hope is in Him.

He truly is my Strength and my Salvation : He is my Defence, so that I shall
not fall.

In GOD is my health, and my glory :
the Rock of my might, and in GOD is my
trust.

O put your trust in Him alway, ye
people : pour out your hearts before Him,
for GOD is our Hope.

As for the children of men, they are
but vanity : the children of men are
deceitful upon the weights, they are
altogether lighter than vanity itself.

O trust not in wrong and robbery, give not yourselves unto vanity : if riches increase, set not your heart upon them.

GOD spake once, and twice I have also heard the same : that power belongeth unto GOD ;

And that Thou, LORD, art merciful : for Thou rewardest every man according to his work.

Glory be to the FATHER, and to the SON : and to the HOLY GHOST ;

As it was in the beginning, is now, and ever shall be : world without end. Amen.

The Witness to the World.

They took knowledge of them that they had been with JESUS.

O THOU, Whom not having seen, I love; in Whom believing, I rejoice; Whose Very Self I have received, and with Whom, by Sacramental Indwelling, I am one; O FATHER, SON, and SPIRIT, Blessed and Eternal LORD, let Thy Grace be with me evermore.

Let me, remembering Whose I am, and with what Price I have been bought, glory in nothing save in the Cross of my LORD JESUS CHRIST, by Whom the world is crucified unto me, and I unto the world.

As with my lips I confess, and with my heart I believe, so in my life let me shew forth the Salvation which Thou hast wrought for sinful man.

Let me, which am CHRIST'S, crucify the flesh with the affections and lusts; let me keep under my body, and bring it into subjection, that though the outward man perish, the inward man may be renewed day by day; bearing about in my body the Dying of the LORD, that the Life also of JESUS may be made manifest in my mortal flesh.

Whatsoever things are true, whatsoever things are honest, whatsoever things are just, whatsoever things are pure, and lovely, and of good report; if there be any virtue, and if there be any praise, let me think on these things.

Let my speech be always with grace, seasoned with salt ; give me fervid zeal, wisdom, charity, and holy discipline.

With meekness let me bear my own burdens, and with charity the burdens of others ; in all things fulfilling the Will of GOD for me, even my sanctification.

May the GOD of Love and Peace be with me, this day and for evermore. Amen.

S. *John* xv. 17.

THESE things I command you, that ye love one another. If the world hate you, ye know that it hated Me before it hated you. If ye were of the world, the world would love his own : but because ye are not of the world, but I have chosen you out of the world, therefore the world hateth you. Remember the word that I said unto you, The servant is not greater than his lord. If they have persecuted Me, they will also persecute you ; if they have kept My saying, they will keep yours also. But all these things will they do unto you for My Name's sake, because they know not Him that sent Me. If I had not come and spoken unto them, they had not had sin : but now they have no cloke for their sin. He that hateth Me hateth My FATHER also. If I had not done among them the works which none other man did, they had not had sin : but now have they both seen and hated both Me and My FATHER. But this cometh to pass, that the word might be fulfilled that is written in their law, They hated Me without a cause. But when the COMFORTER is come, Whom I will send unto you from the FATHER, even the SPIRIT of Truth, Which proceedeth from the FATHER, He shall testify of Me. And ye also shall bear witness, because ye have been with Me from the beginning.

PSALM I.   Beatus bir, qui non abiit.

BLESSED is the man that hath not walked in the counsel of the ungodly, nor stood in the way of sinners : and hath not sat in the seat of the scornful.

But his delight is in the law of the

LORD : and in His law will he exercise himself day and night.

And he shall be like a tree planted by the water-side : that will bring forth his fruit in due season.

His leaf also shall not wither : and look, whatsoever he doeth, it shall prosper.

As for the ungodly, it is not so with them : but they are like the chaff, which the wind scattereth away from the face of the earth.

Therefore the ungodly shall not be able to stand in the judgment : neither the sinners in the congregation of the righteous.

But the LORD knoweth the way of the righteous : and the way of the ungodly shall perish.

Glory be to the FATHER, and to the SON : and to the HOLY GHOST ;

As it was in the beginning, is now, and ever shall be : world without end. Amen.

The Heavenly Life.

Our conversation is in heaven.

GRANT, we beseech Thee, Almighty
GOD, that like as we do believe
Thine Only-begotten SON, our LORD
JESUS CHRIST, to have ascended into the
heavens ; so we may also in heart and
mind thither ascend, and with Him continually dwell, Who liveth and reigneth
with Thee and the HOLY GHOST, One
GOD, world without end.   Amen.

O Blessed High Priest, Holy JESUS,
King of the world and Head of the
Church, Thou hast a feeling for our infirmities, and makest Intercession for us
for ever ; by the virtue of Thine Incarnation, do Thou supply all my wants,
excuse all my infirmities, pity all my sorrows, and send down Thy HOLY SPIRIT
of Grace into my heart, that though I walk
upon the earth, yet my conversation
may be in heaven, and there also may be
my portion and my inheritance for ever.

Hold me by my hand, and keep me, O
Thou Whom my soul loveth ! that where

Thou art, there may Thy servant be. Set me as a seal upon Thy Heart, as a seal upon Thine Arm. Draw me, I will run after Thee. The King hath brought me into His Chambers; this shall be my Rest for ever. Here will I dwell, for I have a delight therein. Amen.

1 *Cor.* i. 4.

I THANK my GOD always on your behalf, for the grace of GOD which is given you by JESUS CHRIST; that in everything ye are enriched by Him, in all utterance, and in all knowledge; even as the testimony of CHRIST was confirmed in you; so that ye come behind in no gift; waiting for the coming of our LORD JESUS CHRIST, Who shall also confirm you unto the end, that ye may be blameless in the day of our LORD JESUS CHRIST.

PSALM XVI. Conserba me, Domine.

PRESERVE me, O GOD: for in Thee have I put my trust.

O my soul, thou hast said unto the LORD: Thou art my GOD, my goods are nothing unto Thee.

All my delight is upon the saints that are in the earth: and upon such as excel in virtue.

But they that run after another god : shall have great trouble.

Their drink-offerings of blood will I not offer : neither make mention of their names within my lips.

The LORD Himself is the portion of mine inheritance, and of my cup : Thou shalt maintain my lot.

The lot is fallen unto me in a fair ground : yea, I have a goodly heritage.

I will thank the LORD for giving me warning : my reins also chasten me in the night-season.

I have set GOD always before me : for He is on my right hand, therefore I shall not fall.

Wherefore my heart was glad, and my glory rejoiced : my flesh also shall rest in hope.

For why? Thou shalt not leave my soul in hell : neither shalt Thou suffer Thy HOLY ONE to see corruption.

Thou shalt shew me the path of life ; in Thy presence is the fulness of joy : and at Thy right hand there is pleasure for evermore.

Glory be to the FATHER, and to the SON : and to the HOLY GHOST ;

As it was in the beginning, is now, and ever shall be : world without end. Amen.

The Sacramental Indwelling.

*The life which I now live in the flesh, I
live by the faith of the SON of GOD.*

ALL praise and glory and thanksgiving be unto Thee, O Blessed LORD
GOD, for the Sacrament of Thy Love,
whereby Thou dwellest in Thy redeemed,
and art their Life and Immortality.

By the grace which Thou hast given to
me, grant me ever to cherish Thy godly
motions, to attend to Thy guidance, and
-to listen to Thy secret whisperings, that
neither in thought, nor word, nor work I
offend Thee.

Let Thy Blessed Image be ever before me, to be copied in me, not by my
own strength or skill, but by Thy SPIRIT
which Thou dost give to them that ask
Thee.

Let me share Thy Obedience by setting
GOD always before me in all things ; Thy
Humility by putting others forward, and
taking the last place myself ; Thy Gentle-
ness by bearing undeserved reproaches
meekly ; Thy Self-Sacrificing Love by

spending and being spent for others. Let me seek Thee in all my actions, in all my thoughts and desires ; let me minister to Thee in Thy sick, Thy poor, Thy little ones. Let me find Thee in prayer, in penitence, in Sacraments of grace. Thus finding Thee, let me at last be found in Thee, and so bid me enter into the Joy of my LORD, exulting in His Presence, and satisfied with His Likeness, and filled for ever and ever with His Fulness, the Fulness of GOD. Amen.

1 *S. John* v. 4

WHATSOEVER is born of GOD overcometh the world ; and this is the victory that overcometh the world, even our faith. Who is he that overcometh the world, but he that believeth that JESUS is the SON of GOD ? This is He that came by water and blood, even JESUS CHRIST ; not by water only, but by water and blood. And it is the SPIRIT that beareth witness, because the SPIRIT is truth. For there are Three that bear record in heaven, the FATHER, the WORD, and the HOLY GHOST : and these Three are One. And there are three that bear witness in earth, the Spirit, and the water, and the blood : and these three agree in one. If we receive the witness of men,

the witness of GOD is greater : for this is
the witness of GOD, which He hath testi-
fied of His SON. He that believeth on
the SON of GOD hath the witness in himself : he that believeth not GOD hath
made Him a liar, because he believeth
not the record that GOD gave of His SON.
And this is the record, that GOD hath
given to us eternal life, and this life is
in His SON. He that hath the SON hath
life ; and he that hath not the SON hath
not life.

PSALM CXXXVIII. Confitebor tibi.

I WILL give thanks unto Thee, O LORD,
with my whole heart : even before
the gods will I sing praise unto Thee.

I will worship toward Thy holy temple,
and praise Thy Name, because of Thy
loving-kindness and truth : for Thou hast
magnified Thy Name, and Thy Word,
above all things.

When I called upon Thee, Thou heard-
est me : and enduedst my soul with much
strength.

All the kings of the earth shall praise
Thee, O LORD : for they have heard the
words of Thy mouth.

Yea, they shall sing in the ways of the
LORD : that great is the glory of the
LORD.

For though the LORD be high, yet hath He respect unto the lowly : as for the proud, He beholdeth them afar off.

Though I walk in the midst of trouble, yet shalt Thou refresh me : Thou shalt stretch forth Thy hand upon the furiousness of mine enemies, and Thy right hand shall save me.

The LORD shall make good His lovingkindness toward me : yea, Thy mercy, O LORD, endureth for ever ; despise not then the works of Thine own hands.

Glory be to the FATHER, and to the SON : and to the HOLY GHOST ;

As it was in the beginning, is now, and ever shall be : world without end. Amen.

An Act of Praise.

Give thanks for a remembrance of His Holiness.

BLESSED art Thou, O LORD GOD, FATHER, SON, and HOLY GHOST; yea, Blessed above all for ever and ever.

We praise Thee, and give thanks to Thee for Thy great glory! Thou alone art, and beside Thee is none other, fully satisfying the hearts which Thou hast created for Thy Praise, Thyself the Light, the Joy, the Life, of them that seek Thee.

We thank Thee for Thy Creating, Redeeming, Sanctifying Love! overflowing the Universe with gladness, making it a temple meet for Thy Praise. Be Thou exalted, LORD, in Thine Own Strength, in all the manifold mysteries of nature and of grace; so will we sing and praise Thy Power. For this Thou hast made us, that we might bless Thy Name, and with our whole being glorify Thee; therefore we give thanks unto Thee, world without end.

Thy Glory is infinite ; Thy Knowledge boundless; Thy Purity awful ; Thy Goodness supreme ; Thy tender Mercies are over all Thy Works, Thy Compassions fail not, and Thou Thyself art Love ; Thou makest Thy Saints to rejoice in Thee, Thou makest them joyful with Glory all Thine Own.

Then suffer me, the least of Thy redeemed, to worship Thee ! Let me praise and exalt Thee in holiness of life, by purity, patience, meekness, and love unfeigned. May Thy Grace overflowing me shew forth to others the riches of Thy Love, that they may glorify GOD in me.

Thou givest us grace that we may be blessed in giving Thee Glory. Thou deignest to accept our praise that Thy Joy may be fulfilled in us. Therefore, my LORD GOD, with all my body and soul and spirit I adore and worship Thee, and give Thee thanks for ever ; Who livest and reignest, GOD Blessed for evermore. Amen.

Col. iii. 12.

PUT on therefore, as the elect of GOD, holy and beloved, bowels of mercies, kindness, humbleness of mind, meekness, long-suffering ; forbearing one another, and forgiving one another, if any man

have a quarrel against any : even as
CHRIST forgave you, so also do ye. And
above all these things put on charity,
which is the bond of perfectness. And
let the peace of GOD rule in your hearts,
to the which also ye are called in one
body ; and be ye thankful. Let the word
of CHRIST dwell in you richly in all
wisdom, teaching and admonishing one
another in psalms, and hymns, and
spiritual songs, singing with grace in
your hearts to the LORD. And whatsoever ye do, in word or deed, do
all in the Name of the LORD JESUS,
giving thanks to GOD and the FATHER
by Him.

PSALM CXLIX. Cantate Domino.

O SING unto the LORD a new song :
let the congregation of saints
praise Him.

Let Israel rejoice in Him that made
him : and let the children of Sion be joyful in their King.

Let them praise His Name in the
dance : let them sing praises unto Him
with tabret and harp.

For the LORD hath pleasure in His
people : and helpeth the meek-hearted.

Let the saints be joyful with glory :
let them rejoice in their beds.

Let the praises of GOD be in their mouth : and a two-edged sword in their hands ;

To be avenged of the heathen : and to rebuke the people ;

To bind their kings in chains : and their nobles with links of iron.

That they may be avenged of them, as it is written : Such honour have all His saints.

PSALM CL. Laudate Dominum.

O PRAISE GOD in His holiness : praise Him in the firmament of His power.

Praise Him in His noble acts : praise Him according to His excellent greatness.

Praise Him in the sound of the trumpet : praise Him upon the lute and harp.

Praise Him in the cymbals and dances : praise Him upon the strings and pipe.

Praise Him upon the well-tuned cymbals : praise Him upon the loud cymbals.

Let everything that hath breath : praise the LORD.

Glory be to the FATHER, and to the SON : and to the HOLY GHOST ;

As it was in the beginning, is now, and ever shall be : world without end. Amen.

The Communion of Saints.

Ye are come unto Mount Sion, and unto the city of the Living GOD, the heavenly Jerusalem, and to an innumerable company of angels, to the general assembly and church of the first-born which are written in heaven, and to GOD the Judge of all, and to the spirits of just men made perfect, and to JESUS, the Mediator of the New Covenant.

JOYS of joys are to thee, thou entire fulness of the saints, blessed Jerusalem, our Mother which art above; keep thou a joyous and unceasing Festival in the peaceful Vision of thy JESUS, the Author of thy freedom.

But chiefest joy be to thee, Mary, singular among Virgins, rose of heavenly sweetness! In Thy SON JESUS do thou alone above all rejoice with joy unspeakable, for He to Whom thou gavest Birth as Man thou adorest as the Living GOD.

Rejoice in the LORD JESUS, your Master, ye Holy Apostles, noble chiefs and princes of heaven, rejoice in Him

Whose Humiliation ye beheld upon earth, with Whom in temptation ye continued, and with Whom as conquerors now ye reign.

Rejoice in JESUS, the Captain of your warfare, ye victorious Martyrs, who now possess, as the Reward of your conflict, Himself for Whom ye gave yourselves to death, JESUS, our GOD.

Rejoice in your Beatitude, ye poor in spirit which reign in heaven ; ye mourners which are comforted ; ye meek which inherit the earth ; ye hungry and thirsty ones whom GOD'S Own Righteousness doth fill. Rejoice, ye merciful, in the mercy of your GOD ; ye pure in heart, whose eyes behold Him ; ye peace-makers, children of the most Mighty Prince of Peace ; ye persecuted saints, for the Kingdom is your own. Rejoice in the LORD alway, and again I say, rejoice !

And thou too, now, lift up thyself, O my soul, with what effort thou canst, and join thyself to the thousands of Saints who rejoice in the LORD. Thither hasten, upborne by faith and love ; there have thy conversation, where CHRIST sitteth at the right hand of GOD.

To Thee, O Blessed JESUS, with the FATHER and the HOLY GHOST, be glory in the Church for ever. For Thou hast loved us, and saved us, and we, O LORD, are Thine.

For us Thou wast made Man, for us wast Crucified, and for us didst Rise again. Thou art gone up on high to prepare a place for us ; and lo ! in the Sacrament of Praise Thou art with us on our Altars, even unto the end of the world. In Thee we live and move and have our being, and share communion with all Saints and with each other, in the fulness of that Life which is the Light of men.

Therefore, making mention of the all-holy, undefiled, and more than Blessed Mary, Ever-Virgin, let us commend ourselves, and one another, and all our life to CHRIST our GOD. Alleluia !

Ephes. ii. 19.

NOW therefore ye are no more strangers and foreigners, but fellow-citizens with the saints, and of the household of GOD ; and are built upon the foundation of the Apostles and Prophets, JESUS CHRIST Himself being the chief Corner-Stone ; in Whom all the building, fitly framed together, groweth unto an holy temple in the LORD : in Whom ye also are builded together for an habitation of GOD, through the SPIRIT.

PSALM CXLVII. **Laubate Dominum.**

O PRAISE the LORD, for it is a good thing to sing praises unto our GOD : yea, a joyful and pleasant thing it is to be thankful.

The LORD doth build up Jerusalem : and gather together the out-casts of Israel.

He healeth those that are broken in heart : and giveth medicine to heal their sickness.

He telleth the number of the stars : and calleth them all by their names.

Great is our LORD, and great is His power : yea, and His wisdom is infinite.

The LORD setteth up the meek : and bringeth the ungodly down to the ground.

O sing unto the LORD with thanksgiving : sing praises upon the harp unto our GOD ;

Who covereth the heaven with clouds, and prepareth rain for the earth : and maketh the grass to grow upon the mountains, and herb for the use of men ;

Who giveth fodder unto the cattle : and feedeth the young ravens that call upon Him.

He hath no pleasure in the strength of an horse : neither delighteth He in any man's legs.

But the LORD'S delight is in them that

fear Him : and put their trust in His mercy.

Praise the LORD, O Jerusalem : praise thy GOD, O Sion.

For He hath made fast the bars of thy gates : and hath blessed thy children within thee.

He maketh peace in thy borders : and filleth thee with the flour of wheat.

He sendeth forth His commandment upon earth : and His word runneth very swiftly.

He giveth snow like wool : and scattereth the hoar-frost like ashes.

He casteth forth His ice like morsels : who is able to abide His frost ?

He sendeth out His word, and melteth them : He bloweth with His wind and the waters flow.

He sheweth His word unto Jacob : His statutes and ordinances unto Israel.

He hath not dealt so with any nation : neither have the heathen knowledge of His laws.

Glory be to the FATHER, and to the SON : and to the HOLY GHOST ;

As it was in the beginning, is now, and ever shall be : world without end. Amen.

A Prayer of Intercession.

I exhort . . . that prayers . . . be made
for all men.

HEAR me, O LORD, while I lift up my voice unto Thee in prayer and supplication for all estates of men in the world and in the Church.

For all Christian Kings, Princes, and Governors, — especially for our own Gracious Sovereign,—that Thou wouldest keep them in the knowledge and fear of Thee, and bring them finally to the Kingdom and the Crown laid up for them in heaven.

For all in Authority in the State, and for all at Court, that they may remember that they are but strangers and pilgrims in this world—citizens of a Heavenly Country.

For all Lawyers and Magistrates ; that they may live in truth and equity, remembering before what Bar they must themselves be judged at the last.

For all Universities, Colleges, and Schools in all Christian lands, that both they who teach and those who are taught, setting the love of Truth before them above all things, may be led to behold it as Thou hast revealed it to man in JESUS CHRIST.

I pray for Thy whole Catholic Church, both Eastern and Western; for all Churches in schism, yet retaining Thy Truth; that they may be one in spirit and in doctrine, and may be restored to visible Communion with each other in Thine Own good time.

For all Reformed Churches; for all heretical communities; that their sin may be pardoned, the sanctity of individuals accepted by Thee, and that they all may be gathered at last into the Fold of Thy Church.

I pray for all Bishops, Priests, and Deacons; that they may feed the Flock of GOD, and win for themselves and for their people crowns of glory from Thy Hand.

Pour out, O LORD, upon the people of England the spirit of devotion. Forgive our negligence of holy things, our irreverence in worship, our tolerance — too often, alas! our love—of error. Save and deliver us, O LORD, who call ourselves a Christian people, from that indifference which is really apostasy, lest we be utterly cut off from Thee at the last.

I pray Thee for all whom Thou hast
called to labour in distant harvest-fields ;
that they may bring home their sheaves
rejoicing.

But more especially I entreat Thee for
the church and congregation to which by
Thy Mercy I belong ; that Thou wouldest
give to all of us increased love and
devotion to Thy Holy Things, an ever-
deepening penitence, an ever-renewed
sanctification of life.

For Thy Priest, my spiritual Father ;
that Thou wouldest regard the Sacrifice
of Thy SON, as offered by him in Thy
Holy Place, and receive his prayers for
his people, and prosper him in all his
ministrations. Be Thou, O LORD, the
very Joy of his heart, and his Portion for
ever.

I pray Thee for all Christian people ;
for the sick, . . . the sad, . . . the sorrowful ; that Thou wouldest make Thyself known unto them in the mystery of
suffering.

I pray Thee in Thy Love to look piti-
fully upon the insane ; deal with them
according to Thy Name, for sweet is Thy
Mercy, and bring them out of darkness
into Light.

For the sinful and the hardened ; for
those who know Thy ways yet walk not
in them ; for those who hear Thy Truth,

yet love it not, and for all who are hastening to their own destruction. Spare, O LORD, and destroy them not! Make their faces ashamed, that they may seek Thy Name.

I pray Thee earnestly for all in doubt, that Thou wouldest touch their hearts with a sense of their great need of Redemption, and so draw them through the Cross unto Thyself.

For all who desire to turn from sin to Thee, yet know not how to repent ; that Thou, O Merciful Absolver, wilt bring them through the Ministry of Reconciliation to the peace and purity which Thou desirest for them.

For all in temptation ; that Thy Strength may be made perfect in their weakness.

I pray Thee for all children—the lambs of Thy Flock ; that Thou wouldest gather them with Thine Arm and carry them in Thy Bosom.

For the dying, that death may be to them the gate of Everlasting Life ; and for all in their last agony, that Thou wouldest Thyself be their Viaticum— their Refreshment by the Way.

I pray Thee for all the faithful whom Thou hast taken hence ; that Thou wouldest grant them forgiveness of all their sins, and a hope full of immortality.

O Thou through Whom are all things, and Who fillest all in all ; receive the prayer of me, an unworthy sinner, for all whom Thou lovest and for whom I desire to pray, in the blessed words which Thy SON Himself hath put into my mouth :

OUR FATHER, Which art in heaven, Hallowed be Thy Name. Thy kingdom come. Thy will be done in earth, As it is in heaven. Give us this day our daily bread. And forgive us our trespasses, As we forgive them that trespass against us. And lead us not into temptation ; But deliver us from evil : For Thine is the kingdom, The power, and the glory, For ever and ever. Amen.

May the Blessing of GOD Almighty, ✠ the FATHER, the SON, and the HOLY GHOST, be upon us, and remain with us for ever. Amen.

Prayers for Special Graces.

For Faith.

ALMIGHTY and Everlasting GOD, Who hast given unto us Thy servants grace by the confession of a true faith to acknowledge the glory of the Eternal TRINITY and in the power of the Divine Majesty to worship the Unity; we beseech Thee that Thou wouldest keep us stedfast in this faith, and evermore defend us from all adversities, Who livest and reignest, one GOD, world without end. Amen.

For Peace of Mind.

ALMIGHTY and Everlasting GOD, Who art always more ready to hear than we to pray, and art wont to give more than either we desire or deserve; pour down upon us the abundance of Thy mercy; forgiving us those things whereof our conscience is afraid, and giving us those good things which we are not worthy to ask, but through the merits and mediation of JESUS CHRIST Thy SON our LORD. Amen.

For Love of God.

O GOD, Who hast prepared for them that love Thee such good things as pass man's understanding ; pour into our hearts such love toward Thee, that we, loving Thee above all things, may obtain Thy promises, which exceed all that we can desire. Through JESUS CHRIST our LORD. Amen.

For Devotion.

LORD of all power and might, Who art the Author and Giver of all good things ; graft in our hearts the love of Thy Name, increase in us true religion, nourish us with all goodness, and of Thy great mercy keep us in the same. Through JESUS CHRIST our LORD. Amen.

For Pardon of Sins.

O LORD, we beseech Thee, absolve Thy people from their offences ; that through Thy bountiful goodness we may all be delivered from the bands of those sins which by our frailty we have committed. Grant this, O Heavenly

FATHER, for JESUS CHRIST'S sake, our
Blessed LORD and SAVIOUR. Amen.

For Acceptance with God.

O GOD, the Strength of all them that
put their trust in Thee, mercifully
accept our prayers ; and because through
the weakness of our mortal nature we can
do no good thing without Thee, grant us
the help of Thy grace, that in keeping
of Thy commandments we may please
Thee, both in will and deed. Through
JESUS CHRIST our LORD. Amen.

For Increased Penitence.

O GOD, from Whom all good things do
come ; mercifully grant unto me
such a measure of contrition as shall be
according to Thy Will ; that I, walking in
the way of obedience, may bring forth
worthy fruits of repentance, to the glory
of Thy Name. Through the grace of
JESUS CHRIST our LORD. Amen.

For Purity.

O GOD, Who by Thy Blessed SON
hast promised the vision of Thy
Glory to the pure in heart ; I pray Thee
so to cleanse my heart from all things
that defile it, that I may at last attain

to Thy Presence wherein is fulness of joy.   Through the same Thy SON, JESUS CHRIST our LORD.   Amen.

For Knowledge.

ALMIGHTY GOD, the Giver of all good gifts, increase in me, I pray Thee, all pure and useful knowledge, and open my understanding day by day to a fuller and deeper apprehension of Thine Immutable Truth which Thou hast revealed to us by the Incarnation of Thy SON, CHRIST our LORD.   Amen.

For Zeal.

O HEAVENLY FATHER, Who with Thine Only-begotten SON givest us freely all things, that thereby we may freely glorify Thee ; give me, I beseech Thee, a fervent zeal in Thy service, that day and night I may minister to Thee, offering in Thy Temple the oblation of myself with great gladness, alway giving praise to Thee, my GOD.   Fill me with a glowing enthusiasm for all good and holy things, that I may never weary of toil, nor repine under trial, nor fail utterly in temptation.   Let all my daily work be consecrate to Thee, that I may do all things to Thy Glory, that my whole heart, and mind,

and soul being set upon the great things
of eternity, I may live above all present
cares, joying in the joy of Thy redeemed,
and fulfilling according to Thy Will Thy
Heart's desire for me, in JESUS CHRIST
our LORD. Amen.

Act of Joy.

HENCEFORTH I will rejoice in the
LORD, henceforth I will give Him
a glad service, I will joy in Him Who is
my only Joy.

O my GOD, what a joy it is to love
Thee ! what joy to feel the length and
breadth and depth of Thy Love shining
in and around me ! Joy in penitence, joy
in sadness, joy in suffering, joy in loneliness.

Thou, O Blessed JESUS, art my Joy, in
Thy Forgiving, Redeeming Love to my
soul.

O HOLY SPIRIT, Thou art my Joy
springing forth from the Heart of the
Divine Love into my heart.

Henceforth I will rejoice in my LORD
GOD, rejoice in doing His Will, rejoice in
living for Him, rejoice in winning souls
for Him, rejoice in yielding up my own
broken being to be made whole by Him,
to the praise and glory of His Holy
Name. Amen.

The Beatitudes.

JESUS opened His mouth and
  taught them, saying,

Blessed are the Poor in Spirit,
    for theirs is the Kingdom of Heaven.

Blessed are they that Mourn,
    for they shall be comforted.

Blessed are the Meek,
    for they shall inherit the earth.

Blessed are they which do hunger and
    thirst after Righteousness,
    for they shall be filled.

Blessed are the Merciful,
    for they shall obtain mercy.

Blessed are the Pure in Heart,
    for they shall see GOD.

Blessed are the Peacemakers,
    for they shall be called the children
    of GOD.

Blessed are they which are persecuted
    for Righteousness' sake,
    for theirs is the Kingdom of Heaven.

A Rule of Life.

' Yield yourselves unto GOD, as those that are alive from the dead, and your bodies as instruments of righteousness unto GOD.'

Seek to give GOD glory

1. In body, by pure behaviour.
2. In soul, by devout communion.
3. In spirit, by intelligent service.

Strive, with GOD'S grace, to resist temptation

1. In thought, by earnest prayer.
2. In word, by prudent reticence.
3. In deed, by lowly self-denial.

Endeavour to imitate JESUS CHRIST.

1. His Obedience, in doing GOD's Will.
2. His Humility, in bearing reproach.
3. His Love, in winning souls.

' Grow in grace and in the Knowledge of our LORD and SAVIOUR JESUS CHRIST. To Him be glory both now and for ever.'

Edinburgh University Press:

T. AND A. CONSTABLE, PRINTERS TO HER MAJESTY.

www.ingramcontent.com/pod-product-compliance
Lightning Source LLC
Chambersburg PA
CBHW020537270326
41927CB00006B/620